GRAB LIFE BY
THE BALLS

*What to Do When Life Falls Apart
and You're the Only One Who Can Fix It*

Author

RONALD D. HALL

Dedication

For the ones who lost themselves trying to live by someone else's script, this book is your permission slip to come back home to yourself.

Acknowledgments

This book was not written in isolation. It carries the fingerprints of every conversation, breakdown, and breakthrough I've ever witnessed. To the people who trusted me with their stories, who taught me through their pain and their resilience, you are the reason these pages exist.

And to the readers: your willingness to face your own truth is the only acknowledgment this work will ever need.

TABLE OF CONTENTS

PREFACE

You don't need another book filled with clichés, empty affirmations, or surface-level hacks. You've tried those already and they didn't work.

This book isn't about balance, gratitude journals, or pretending everything is fine. It's about calling out the lies you've been living, confronting the weight you've been carrying and reclaiming the parts of you that were never broken- only buried.

If you're tired of disappearing in your own life, if you're angry at how the rules were written, if you're ready to stop performing and start participating, this is your entry point.

This isn't self-help. This is self-return

CHAPTER ONE

THE DAY YOU WENT MISSING

"The soul becomes dyed with the colour of its thoughts."
Marcus Aurelius

For the high-functioning person who's quietly falling apart: This isn't self-help. This is self-return.

THE NUMBNESS

You don't know what to do next.
Not really.

- You wake up.

- You check your phone: 43 notifications you don't care about.

- You stare at the wall.

- You go through the motions.

- Maybe you make it to work.

- Maybe you even crack a joke in the morning Slack huddle.

But you're not really here.
You've become a ghost in your own life.

You laugh at memes without feeling them.
You hug people without warmth.
You plan your week and forget what day it is.
You sit in your car in the parking lot after work
scrolling Instagram, watching other people's highlight reels,
and realize you've been sitting there for 20 minutes
to avoid going home to your own life.

You've tried everything.
Morning routines that made you feel like a robot going through the motions.
Productivity apps that turned your life into a video game you're losing.
Gratitude journals where you write the same three things every day
because you can't think of anything else to be thankful for.
Self-care Sunday that feels like another item on your to-do list.

You've listened to podcasts while sitting in traffic, about
"optimizing your potential"
wondering why your potential
feels like a debt you can never pay off.

But the heaviness doesn't care about your life hacks.
It lingers.

Not because you're lazy.
Not because you're ungrateful.
But because you've been carrying a weight for so long
you don't remember what lightness feels like anymore.

You didn't lose yourself all at once.
You disappeared slowly,
by being everything to everyone but you.

You were sold a lie.

Work hard, they said. Follow the rules. Be grateful for what you have.
Keep your head down, pay your dues, and someday it'll all make sense.

Bullshit.

You did everything right and you're still running on empty.
You climbed the ladder before you realized it was leaning against the wrong wall.
You played by their rules and the game was rigged from the start.

And now you're standing in your life,
same walls, same people, same routine,
wondering when you became a stranger to yourself.

THE COLLAPSE

It doesn't start with screaming.
It starts with checking your email at 11:47 PM
because your anxiety won't let you sleep
until you know what fresh hell awaits you tomorrow.

It starts with buying things you don't need
because the shopping cart dopamine hit
is the only joy you can manufacture.

It starts with ghosting friends
because explaining how you feel
is more exhausting than isolation.

It starts with refreshing LinkedIn
wondering if everyone else got the memo
about how to actually enjoy their career.

THE EXECUTIVE WHO VANISHED

I worked with a man who ran a multi-million-dollar company.
Corner office. Six-figure salary. Stock options.
The American Dream on paper.

He told me he knew he was done
when he found himself staring at a blinking cursor for five hours,
writing the same quarterly report he'd written 20 times before,
while his assistant knocked to remind him about a meeting
he'd completely blanked on.

"I kept hearing people walk by," he said.
"They thought I was working.
I wasn't even breathing right.
I was just... gone."

Here's what high-functioning collapse looks like:

- You dread Sunday evenings more than you enjoy Friday nights

- You refresh social media compulsively, then feel worse about your life

- You say "I'm fine" while your chest feels like it's caving in

- You avoid mirrors because you don't recognize who's looking back

- You buy self-help books you never finish because reading about change is   easier than changing

- You fantasize about disappearing (not dying, just leaving your responsibilities behind, walking away)

- You're tired of being grateful for scraps while watching others feast

This isn't about weakness.
This is about being pissed off.
And you should be.

You were told that hard work pays off.
That following the rules leads to fulfillment.
That if you just keep grinding, someday you'll "make it."

They lied.

The system is designed to keep you exhausted,
distracted, and grateful for breadcrumbs
while the people who wrote the rules
live off the loaf you helped them bake.

You're not broken.
You're reacting normally to an abnormal situation.

THE MIRROR

Here's what no one tells you—
Sometimes your breakdown looks like success.
Sometimes it looks like responsibility.
Sometimes it looks like being really, really good at pretending.

People don't ask if you're okay
when you still make your deadlines.
They don't check on you
if your Zoom camera is on and you're nodding at the right
moments.
They don't know you're unraveling
because you've learned how to bleed without making a mess.

Just because you're functioning doesn't mean you're fine.
It means you've learned how to suffer efficiently.

You don't need another productivity hack.
You don't need another motivational Instagram quote.
You don't need to "find balance" in a system designed to drain you.

You need to get angry.
Really, properly angry.

You need a mirror that doesn't flinch when you look into it.

Because here's the brutal truth–
You've been abandoning yourself for so long
you started calling it "discipline."

Every time you say yes when you mean no.
Every time you shrink to keep the peace.
Every time you silence your rage to make others comfortable.
Every time you apologize for taking up space.
Every time you convince yourself you're "lucky to have a job"
when that job is slowly killing your soul.

You've abandoned yourself so efficiently,
you convinced yourself it was maturity.

Let me say this bluntly:

If you're snapping at people who didn't hurt you,
If you keep forgetting to eat real meals,
If you wake up with dread in your chest before your feet hit the floor,
If you binge-scroll at 2 AM because your brain won't shut off,
If your joy feels fake and your peace feels forced,
If you're tired of being told to "practice gratitude" when you're drowning–

You're not crazy.
You're not weak.
You're not broken.

You're pissed off.
And it's about damn time.

THE RAGE YOU'RE NOT SUPPOSED TO FEEL

They told you to be grateful.
They told you others have it worse.
They told you to focus on the positive.

But what about your anger?
What about your right to be furious
that you did everything they asked
and still feel empty?

What about the rage of realizing
you've been performing a version of success
that was never designed for you?

What about being pissed off
that "work-life balance" is a myth
sold to people who are too tired to demand better?

Your anger isn't the problem.
Your anger is information.

It's telling you that something is wrong.
It's telling you that you deserve more
than surviving your own life.
It's telling you that the rules you followed
were written by people who profit from your compliance.

You have every right to be angry.

At the job that demands your soul for a paycheck.
At the culture that calls exhaustion "hustle."
At the system that convinces you that your worth
is measured by your productivity.
At yourself for believing it for so long.

THE RE-ENTRY

You've been surviving.
And let's be clear—
that was an achievement.

You made it through things that should have shattered you.
You held it together when no one else noticed.
You built a life out of broken parts
and kept walking when your soul wanted to stop.

But survival isn't the destination.
It was the bridge.
And now it's time to cross over.

Don't confuse resilience with self-abandonment.
Just because you got through it doesn't mean you're okay.

Let's talk about coming home to yourself.

Not a mystical journey.
Not a wellness retreat.
Not another self-optimization project.

I'm talking about the moment you stop performing
and start participating.
The moment you stop editing your pain
to make it digestible for others.
The moment you stop apologizing
for wanting more than scraps.

The moment you say:
"I don't know who I am anymore...
but I'm ready to find out.
And I'm done pretending this is enough."

FOUR STEPS TO TAKING YOUR LIFE BACK

Here's the path to walk:

1. **CONFRONT** the lies you've been living and the system that sold them to you.

2. **UNLEARN** the toxic definitions of success, strength, and worth that are killing you.

3. **RECLAIM** the parts of you that were never broken, only buried under expectations.

4. **REBUILD** a life that serves you. Period.

Every chapter unpacks these layers.

No nonsense.

No spiritual bypassing.

No toxic positivity.

Just depth. Truth. Revolution.

You've spent your life making others comfortable.

This is the time to set yourself free.

THE CHALLENGE

You've made it through the first door.

You've named what's been unspoken.

You've looked in the mirror and told the truth,

even if just in a whisper.

For certainty:

You didn't come here to collect inspirational quotes.

You came here because something inside you won't shut up anymore.

You're tired of disappearing in your own life.

You're tired of performing while no one sees the panic behind your smile.

You're tired of being told to "just keep going"
when you don't even know where you're headed.

So don't stop here.

Challenge Yourself!

Don't turn the next page until you've done this:

1. **Write down the moment you realized you were living someone else's definition of success.**

   The moment you knew the game was rigged.
   The moment you felt the crack in your foundation.
   Name it. Own it.

2. **List the masks you wear to survive your own life.**

   The "I'm fine" mask.
   The "I'm grateful" mask.
   The "I've got it all together" mask.
   Write them down. Then burn the list.

3. **Say this out loud, where it echoes:**

   "I'm angry. I'm tired. And I'm done pretending this is enough."
   That sound?
   That's your voice returning.

The world doesn't need more people pretending to be fine.
It needs more people telling the truth.
And that starts with you.

You didn't lose your fire.
You just buried it under survival.
It's still there.
Flickering.
Waiting.

You don't have to feel ready.
You just have to stay.
Here.
In this moment.
In this version of you who hasn't given up yet.

You've survived.
Now let's teach your bones how to rise.

It won't be comfortable.
But comfort isn't the goal.
Freedom is.

We don't fix ourselves here.
We free ourselves.

No applause.
No filters.
No pretending.

Just a voice like yours,
and a life worth reclaiming.

CHAPTER TWO

OWN YOUR INNER WAR

"The loudest battles are the ones no one else hears."
Author Unknown

THE WAR BENEATH THE SKIN

You want to know what really breaks people?

It's not just loss. Not just trauma. Not just failure.

It's lying awake at 2 AM scrolling your phone because sleep means reprieve but you can't get there.

Your thoughts saying "I'm fine", and meaning it, when you're falling apart inside, because you've convinced yourself this is just how life feels.

It's researching new careers on Indeed during lunch breaks but never applying because "what's the point?"

It's the voice inside your head that narrates every moment with doubt, every silence with shame, and every setback with the sentence: "See? I knew you'd mess up."

That's the real war. Not the job. Not the bills. Not even the past.

It's the constant inner dialogue that tells you you're not enough, loudest when you're most alone.

You could be getting promoted, getting married, getting praised on LinkedIn, but if the voice in your head is saying "you're a fraud," none of it matters.

Because the battle is inside and the enemy? It knows your name. It knows your fears. It knows how to sound like you when it's trying to tear you down.

You're not defeated. You've just been backing the voice that wants you broken.

Here's what nobody tells you about being stuck

You've read the books. You've tried the morning routines. You've downloaded the meditation apps and bought the journals with the inspirational covers.

And you're tired of being tired of trying.

You're tired of advice that assumes you can just "follow your passion" when you're two paychecks from homelessness.

You're tired of success stories from people who had safety nets you never had.

You're tired of being told to "think positive" when your reality genuinely sucks.

This chapter is where we stop pretending we're just "overthinking." This is where we stop saying "I'm just hard on myself." This is where we get honest about the **self-sabotage**, **self-rejection**, and **mental warfare** that's been keeping you stuck.

Not because you're broken. But because somewhere along the line, you learned to protect yourself by turning on yourself.

Dr. Kristin Neff (Self-Compassion Researcher): "We've been taught that beating ourselves up is the way to be strong. But self-criticism only fuels shame. And shame shuts down growth."

So here's the truth—

If you want to change your life, you have to start by changing how you speak to yourself when no one else is listening.

THE VOICE YOU INHERITED

Let's talk about that voice in your head.

You know the one. It tells you you're not ready. That you're too much. Or not enough. That you'll embarrass yourself if you try. That if people really knew you, they'd walk away.

You think it's *your* voice, but it's not. Not all of it.

That voice has ancestors. That voice has fingerprints.

It sounds like you now because you've been rehearsing it for years. But if you trace it back, you'll find someone else at the beginning.

A parent who shamed you for crying. A teacher who only noticed when you failed. A friend who made you feel like too much. A world that told you strength meant silence. A religion that confused fear with virtue. A culture that rewards burnout and calls it ambition.

The brutal truth—

You didn't wake up one day and decide to hate yourself. You absorbed it. You inherited it. You learned to speak to yourself the way others spoke to you, or about you.

And then, somewhere along the way, you mistook their voice for your own.

Take Note

The voice in your head was born in someone else's mouth.

Let's go deeper.

Think back. Who were you before you learned to perform?

Before you learned to shrink to be safe? Before you thought silence was strength? Before you started apologizing for your existence? Before you became the person who says "sorry" when someone else bumps into you?

That version of you isn't gone. It's just buried under years of criticism disguised as love and pressure.

This is where healing begins— not with affirmations, but with audits.

You have to **audit your beliefs.** Who taught you to doubt yourself? Whose approval are you still chasing with your silence? Who do you become when you're scared?

Reflection

When you hear the words "You're not enough," whose voice is that? Whose face flashes through your memory? What moment still echoes when you doubt yourself?

This isn't about blame. This is about **ownership.**

Because as long as you believe that voice is you, you'll keep obeying it.

But once you name it, once you call it out, you get to reclaim your authority.

Dr. Nicole LePera (The Holistic Psychologist) says: "Much of your internal narrative is borrowed. Healing means learning to return what was never yours."

That's the work we're doing now. We're returning what was never ours to carry. The shame. The doubt. The belief that you have to earn love by shrinking.

Let me tell you something hard and beautiful.

You're allowed to break up with the version of you that existed just to be accepted.

You're allowed to stop performing. You're allowed to say no. You're allowed to rewrite everything that was written in fear.

The Pastor's Daughter

She was the oldest child. Smart. Sweet. A peacemaker. She learned early that "good girls" don't make waves. They smile. They serve. They sacrifice.

By the time she was 28, she couldn't make a decision without a panic attack. She'd internalized her entire worth as being liked, useful, invisible.

We sat in silence one day, and she said:

"I don't think I know what I want. I only know what would make people happy."

That's what this chapter is about. That's what this war is. It's not just about pain. It's about identity.

Because when you inherit a voice long enough, you don't just obey it. You become it.

Let's undo that.

Let's return what was never yours and pick up what always was.

Your voice, your truth, your yes, your no. Your name spoken without apology.

Healing begins where obedience ends.

THE REALITY CHECK NOBODY GIVES YOU

Before we talk about changing your inner dialogue, let's acknowledge something the motivational speakers won't.

You're not just fighting internal battles. You're fighting while drowning in obligations.

You can't just "follow your bliss" when you've got:

- Student loan payments that will outlive you
- A mortgage or rent that eats half your paycheck
- Kids who need stability, not your quarter-life crisis
- Parents aging faster than your savings account grows
- A resume gap that screams questions you can't answer

The comparison trap is real. Everyone else seems to have it figured out. LinkedIn is full of "I quit my corporate job to follow my dreams" posts. Instagram shows you people your age buying houses, traveling, starting businesses.

Meanwhile, you're googling "is it normal to cry in your car after work" and clearing your search history.

Here's what they don't show you–

- The trust funds behind the "I took a leap" stories
- The partners carrying the financial load during "brave" career changes
- The privilege of having family money as a safety net
- The depression behind the highlight reels

Your struggle isn't a character flaw. It's a system problem dressed up as a personal failing.

But here's the thing: **You still have to work within your reality.**

This isn't about waiting for the perfect moment to change your life. It's about changing your relationship with the life you have while you're building something better.

Take note

You've been both the prisoner and the warden. Time to stage a jailbreak.

SILENT SABOTAGE: THE DAILY REALITY

There's a kind of self-destruction that doesn't look dramatic. It doesn't involve rock bottom. It doesn't make the news.

It looks like this:

- You don't apply for the job you want because you assume they'll say no

- You answer "whatever you want" when someone asks what you need, because you stopped believing you're allowed to want anything

- You finish a task and immediately criticize yourself for not doing it better

- You get close to someone emotionally and then pull away because intimacy feels dangerous

- You make a mistake and mentally punish yourself for the rest of the week

- You research solutions to your problems but never actually implement them

- You start projects with enthusiasm but abandon them the moment they get difficult

- You say "I should probably..." about the same things for months without acting

- You fake being busy to avoid conversations about your future

- You scroll social media when you're supposed to be working, then hate yourself for procrastinating

The Sunday Night Spiral: Every week, same routine. Sunday evening hits and the dread settles in. Another week of the same job, same problems, same stuck feeling. You promise yourself Monday will be different. Monday comes. Nothing changes. By Wednesday, you've forgotten you ever wanted change.

This is what silent sabotage looks like. It's a slow erosion of your own potential, carried out by the version of you that still believes survival means staying small.

Self-sabotage isn't failure. It's fear in disguise.

Let's break it down. Most people stuck in self-sabotage are caught in this cycle:

1. **Desire** — You feel pulled toward something. A dream. A change. A risk.

2. **Doubt** — The voice chimes in: "Who do you think you are?"

3. **Delay** — You hesitate, overthink, analyze. You find reasons to wait.

4. **Distraction** — You scroll. You binge. You get busy with anything else.

5. **Despair** — You beat yourself up for procrastinating. Shame kicks in.

6. **Repeat** — The next opportunity? You trust yourself even less.

Sound familiar?

It's not that you're incapable. It's that you've spent years unconsciously rehearsing this cycle. And like anything practiced, it became automatic.

Dr. Caroline Leaf (Neuroscientist): "Every time you have a thought, you build a real, physical structure in your brain. Repeated thoughts become highways."

Your inner war is built on well-traveled roads: Shame highways. Doubt highways. Fear highways.

We're not going to "affirm" our way out of this. We're going to bulldoze the roads and build new ones.

COMMON SILENT SABOTAGE PATTERNS

◆ **Perfectionism** You delay starting anything because it has to be flawless. If it's not? You'd rather never begin.

Truth: Perfection is procrastination with good PR.

◆ **People-Pleasing** You say yes when you mean no. You become who others need, even if it means losing who you are.

Truth: People-pleasing is self-abandonment dressed up as kindness.

◆ **Procrastination** You call yourself lazy, but that's not it. You're overwhelmed or afraid. Or convinced you'll fail anyway.

Truth: Procrastination is often a trauma response, not a character flaw.

◆ **Overcommitting** You stay busy to avoid your own feelings. You stack your calendar so you never have to be still.

Truth: Constant busyness is a socially acceptable way to avoid dealing with the hard stuff.

◆ **Analysis Paralysis** You research everything to death but never take action. You have seventeen tabs open about starting a business but haven't written a single business plan.

Truth: Information without implementation is just procrastination on life support.

Ask yourself: Which pattern shows up most in you? What is it protecting you from?

Write it. Don't think it. Write it.

The Artist Who Didn't Create

He had a gift. Everyone said so. But he hadn't painted in three years.

He said it was because he didn't have time. The truth? He was terrified that if he tried and it wasn't perfect, he'd lose the one thing that made him feel valuable.

So he protected the illusion by never creating at all.

That's how sabotage works. It hides inside logic. It disguises itself as practicality. But underneath? It's fear, dressed like reason.

You can't fight what you don't name. So we name it. We write it. We hold it to the light. And then we do the bravest thing of all– We keep moving ahead anyway.

Your potential didn't die. It's just being held hostage by your fear.

THE TURNING POINT

There comes a moment in every internal war where you realize the enemy is just an echo, a loud one, a convincing one, but not the truth.

That moment? It doesn't feel like victory. It feels like grief.

Because when you finally hear the inner critic clearly, you realize how long you've been obeying it.

You think:

- "I've spent years living by rules I didn't write."
- "I've called myself names I wouldn't use on a stranger."
- "I've stayed small so other people wouldn't feel uncomfortable."
- "I've apologized for things that weren't my fault."
- "I've made myself invisible to avoid judgment."

And it hits you: the war wasn't just hard. It was lonely.

Because for so long, you've been fighting yourself without even realizing it.

Take Note

The inner critic is loud. But it isn't wise. It's as old as you are. And it's scared.

THE INNER CRITIC ISN'T YOU – IT'S A PART OF YOU

Internal Family Systems (IFS) therapy, pioneered by Dr. Richard Schwartz, teaches us:

We aren't one voice. We're many.

And some of those voices were formed to keep us safe when we were vulnerable. They are parts of us: protective, wounded, frozen in time.

The Four Core Parts We'll Work With:

1. **The Critic** — The voice that shames. "You're not enough. You never get it right."

2. **The Protector** — The one that avoids risk. "Just stay quiet. Don't make it worse."

3. **The Child** — The version of you that first felt afraid, abandoned, or unseen.

4. **The Witness** — The part of you that sees things clearly. The one we're trying to strengthen.

You don't kill the critic; you understand it. You don't silence the child; you sit with it. You don't banish the protector; you thank it and let it rest. From that place, your **witness self**, you start to rewrite the story.

THE REWRITE BEGINS WITH RECOGNITION

Before we get to solutions, you first need to acknowledge yourself in the struggle.

You're the person who:

- Says "I'm fine" when you're falling apart inside

- Googles "how to know if you're depressed" at 3 AM but never follows through

- Feels like everyone else got a manual for adulthood that you never received

- Compares your behind-the-scenes to everyone else's highlight reel

- Has conversations with yourself that you'd never let anyone else hear

- Feels guilty for wanting more when you know others have less

- Thinks there's something fundamentally wrong with you because happiness feels so hard
- Wonders if this is just how adult life feels: empty, exhausting, endless

You're also the person who:

- Shows up for everyone else but forgets to show up for yourself
- Has survived things you never talk about
- Keeps going even when everything inside you wants to quit
- Cares so deeply it hurts
- Has more strength than you give yourself credit for

Take Note

You're not broken. You're just tired of carrying everyone else's expectations of who you should be and letting others' expectations become your own.

REWRITING THE SCRIPT

You've listened to the inner critic long enough. You know how it talks: like shame in a suit, like fear with a clipboard, like a parent who only praised you when you were quiet and obedient.

Now it's time to hand the pen to someone else, to the part of you that remembers who you were before survival taught you to shrink.

This isn't about thinking positive. It's about thinking truthfully.

There's a difference.

You don't need to silence your inner critic. You need to outnumber it with better voices.

BUILD YOUR INNER TEAM

Let's build those voices - on purpose. These aren't fantasies. They are versions of you you've buried, neglected, or never met.

◆ **The Truth-Teller** This voice doesn't hype you up. It reminds you what's real. "You've survived 100% of your worst days so far." "You don't owe anyone your silence." "You were never meant to be a watered-down version of yourself." "Your worth isn't determined by your productivity."

◆ **The Inner Guardian** This voice doesn't ask for permission. It sets boundaries. It protects your peace. "I'm not available for self-betrayal anymore." "That may have worked before. But it doesn't fly here." "No is a complete sentence." "I don't have to explain my healing to anyone."

◆ **The Practical Strategist** This voice acknowledges your real constraints while finding workable solutions. "We can't quit tomorrow, but we can start building something on the side." "Small steps count. Imperfect action beats perfect inaction." "We're playing a long game here."

◆ **The Future Self** This isn't fantasy. This is the version of you who's done the work, who knows how far you've come. Ask: "What did you have to let go of to become real?" Then write that list. That's your next step.

THE REFRAME LOOP

Let's put it into practice. Take one core belief that's been keeping you stuck and walk it through:

Step 1: Name the Original Belief

"If I speak up, I'll lose people."

Step 2: Trace the Origin

"When did I first learn this?" "Whose voice do I hear?" "What situation taught me this was 'true'?"

Step 3: Challenge It

"Is this always true?" "What evidence proves otherwise?" "Who benefits from me believing this?" "What's the cost of continuing to believe this?"

Step 4: Reframe It

"I don't lose people when I speak up. I lose people who can't handle my truth, and that's not a loss. That's alignment."

More Reframes for Common Beliefs:

Old: "I'm not qualified enough." **New:** "I'm learning as I go, just like everyone else."

Old: "I should be further along by now." **New:** "I'm exactly where I need to be to learn what I need to learn."

Old: "I don't have time to change my life." **New:** "I don't have time NOT to change my life. This is it."

Old: "What if I fail?" **New:** "What if I succeed? And what if failure just means I learned something?"

James Clear, *Atomic Habits*: "Every action you take is a vote for the type of person you want to become."

What you say to yourself is also a vote. So stop casting ballots for shame.

The Teen Who Decided to Matter

He was 17. Lived in a house where being invisible kept him safe. His dad didn't listen. His mom shut down.

So he stopped speaking up. For years.

> Until one day, he sent himself a voice message. Just one shaky sentence:
>
> "I'm allowed to matter. Even if no one's listening."
>
> He played it back every morning. Two years later, he's mentoring other young men, not with speeches, but with presence.

That's how fast the script can flip when you stop waiting for someone else to write it.

You've met the enemy. Not outside you – inside.

You've called it what it is – the inner war. Not a flaw. Not a diagnosis. Not just "overthinking." A survival instinct that overstayed its welcome.

Now it's time to decide:

Do you keep obeying the old script, or begin writing the one that fits who you're becoming?

Not who you were. Not who they needed you to be. Not the role you played to survive.

But the version of you that isn't ashamed to speak truth, set boundaries, and stop apologizing for being here.

> **Take Note**
>
> Stop being your own worst enemy and start being your own best advocate.

> **THE CHALLENGE**

Don't move to Chapter Three until you've done these. Yes, they're uncomfortable. That's the point. Breakthroughs don't happen through comfort. They happen through courage.

1. Write a Letter to Your Inner Critic.

Don't censor. Don't be polite.

Say what needs to be said:

- "You don't get to run my life anymore."

- "You protected me once. But now you're hurting me."

- "I'm not letting fear masquerade as wisdom."

- "Your job was to keep me safe when I was small. I'm not small anymore."

Read it aloud. Even if your voice shakes. Especially if it does.

2. Speak the New Script

Find a quiet place. No mirror needed. No theatrics. Just say this:

"I've betrayed myself for the last time. I've let fear write my story, and shame direct the scenes. But I am the author now. And I say: I am worthy. I am enough. I am not small. I get to take up space. I get to speak up. I get to come home to myself. I get to want things and work toward them. I get to fail and try again. I get to be human."

Say it again tomorrow. Say it when you're doubting everything. Say it until it starts to feel true.

3. Tell Someone One Honest Thing

Pick one person you trust. And say something you've never said before.

It could be:

- "I've been really lost lately."

- "I'm scared all the time, and I hide it well."

- "I don't know who I am without performing."

- "I feel like I've been pretending for so long, I don't know how to stop."

- "I'm tired of being tired."

This is your declaration. This is how wars end – with honesty.

4. Identify Your Next Small Step

Don't plan your whole life transformation. Just identify ONE thing you can do this week that honors who you're becoming:

- Apply for one job that scares you
- Say no to one obligation that drains you
- Start one conversation you've been avoiding
- Take one action you've been researching but never implementing

Carl Jung: "Until you make the unconscious conscious, it will direct your life and you will call it fate."

You've made the unconscious conscious. You've called out the sabotage. You've started to remember who you are.

Now build a life around that truth.

Resilience isn't pretending everything's fine. Resilience is what happens when you stop abandoning yourself during the hard moments and start showing up with compassion, clarity, and courage.

You've fought the internal war. You've named the voice. You've picked up the pen.

Now it's time to build the core that can carry everything that comes next.

You don't win the inner war by being louder. You win it by thinking differently.

You've listened. You've spoken.

Welcome to the other side.

CHAPTER THREE

REAL RESILIENCE

"Resilience isn't about being bulletproof. It's about bleeding with purpose."
Author Unknown

THE 2 AM GOOGLE SEARCH

It's Tuesday night. You're lying in bed, scrolling your phone because sleep feels impossible. Your mind is racing through tomorrow's meetings, this month's bills, and that conversation you keep avoiding.

So you do what millions of people do– You google "how to quit your life."

Not your job. Your *life*.

Because somewhere between paying the mortgage and pretending everything's fine, you lost yourself. And now you're wondering if this grinding, exhausting, soul-crushing routine is all there is.

Here's what I want you to know– You're not having a midlife crisis. You're having a truth emergency.

And that's exactly where real resilience begins.

WHAT THEY GOT WRONG ABOUT STRENGTH

THE LIE: "Suck it up. Push through. Don't let them see you sweat."

THE TRUTH: That's not strength. That's slow-motion self-destruction with a good work ethic.

You've been performing strength for so long, you forgot what the real thing feels like. Real strength isn't about never breaking down. It's about not abandoning yourself when you do.

Let me guess what "strength" looked like in your house growing up:

- Don't cry (especially if you're a man)
- Don't complain
- Don't stop moving
- Don't need anyone
- Don't feel too much

Sound familiar?

That's not resilience. That's emotional repression with a productivity obsession.

Real resilience looks like this:

- Saying "I'm not okay" when you're not okay
- Taking a mental health day without guilt
- Asking for help before you're drowning
- Setting boundaries that protect your energy
- Crying in your car and then going back inside

THE SUNDAY SCARIES ARE REAL

Every Sunday around 4 PM, it hits you. That sinking feeling in your stomach. The dread creeping up your spine. Tomorrow is Monday and you have to put the mask back on.

Smile at the coworkers who drain you. Sit in meetings that could have been emails. Pretend you care about quarterly reports when your soul is screaming for something real.

You're not broken. You're just tired of living someone else's definition of success.

The Sunday Scaries aren't a personal failing. They're your inner truth detector going off. Your body is trying to tell you something. Are you listening?

THE OFFICE WARRIOR WHO FINALLY CRACKED

Sarah was the "reliable one." Never missed a deadline. Always said yes. Worked weekends without complaint.

At 34, she was promoted to manager. More money, more responsibility, more reasons to stay grateful and quiet.

But every morning, she sat in her car for ten minutes before going inside. Just breathing. Just preparing to pretend.

One Tuesday, she didn't get out of the car.

She sat there for an hour, crying, googling "therapists near me" on her phone.

Her friends called it a breakdown.

I call it a breakthrough.

Because that was the day she stopped abandoning herself for a paycheck.

Sarah's turning point – "I realized I wasn't having panic attacks. I was having truth attacks. My body was trying to save me from a life I didn't actually want."

THE 90-SECOND RULE (YOUR NEW SURVIVAL TOOL)

Here's something they don't teach you in corporate training–

When you feel overwhelmed, your body floods with stress chemicals. But here's the science: That chemical reaction only lasts 90 seconds.

Everything after that? That's your mind replaying the story.

Try this right now:

1. Feel that tightness in your chest or jaw
2. Set a timer for 90 seconds
3. Breathe into the feeling (don't fight it)
4. Name it: "This is anxiety. This is frustration. This is grief."
5. Watch what happens when the timer goes off

You're not "too sensitive." You're just untrained in letting emotions pass through instead of building a fortress around them.

Pro tip: Do this in bathroom stalls, parked cars, or supply closets. Wherever you can get 90 seconds of truth.

WHAT YOUR BODY IS TRYING TO TELL YOU

Your body keeps the score. Every deadline you dreaded. Every conversation you avoided. Every time you said "fine" when you meant "dying inside."

It shows up as:

- Headaches that won't quit
- Jaw-clenching during Zoom calls
- Insomnia when you're exhausted

- Getting sick more often

- That weird chest tightness when your boss texts you at 9 PM

Your body isn't broken. It's trying to protect you.

But you can't live in armor and expect to feel free.

THE PARENT TRAP (WHEN EVERYONE NEEDS YOU)

You're juggling aging parents and demanding kids. Your partner needs support. Your boss needs "just five more minutes." Your friends need someone to listen.

Everyone's cup is full except yours.

The lie they sold you: "Good people sacrifice themselves for others."

The truth: You can't pour from an empty cup, and martyrdom isn't a personality trait.

Mark's wake-up call: The 42-year-old dad who realized he was teaching his kids that love means disappearing. "I wanted to show them how to be strong, but I was actually showing them how to vanish."

His new rule: "I can't be everyone's superhero if I'm my own villain."

BOUNDARIES ARE NOT WALLS

Let's clear this up: Setting boundaries doesn't make you selfish. It makes you sustainable.

Boundaries sound like:

- "I don't check emails after 7 PM"

- "I need 20 minutes to decompress when I get home"

- "I can't take on another project right now"

- "I love you, but I can't fix this for you"

- "Let me get back to you on that"

Not walls. Doors. Doors that let the right things in and keep the wrong things out.

The boundary that changed everything: "I stopped explaining my 'no.' No is a complete sentence."

THE CAREER PIVOT AT 38

James had the golden handcuffs. Great salary, corner office, respect from colleagues. On paper, he'd "made it."

In reality, he spent his commute fantasizing about quitting. Every promotion felt like a prettier prison cell.

At 38, he made a list:

*Things that drain my soul

*Things that make me feel alive

*What I'd do if money wasn't a factor

That list changed his life. Not overnight. But one decision at a time.

James now: "I make less money, but I sleep better. Turns out, peace of mind has a price tag, and I was paying way too much for misery."

YOUR RESILIENCE EMERGENCY KIT

Keep these tools handy for when life hits sideways.

1. The Two-Minute Reset

- Name what you're feeling out loud

- Take five deep breaths

- Ask: "What do I need right now?"

- Give yourself permission to need it

2. The Energy Audit

Weekly check-in:

- What gave me energy this week?

- What drained it?

- What can I do less of?

- What do I need more of?

3. The Truth Text

Find one person who can handle your reality. Text them when you're struggling. Don't perform. Just be real.

Example: "Having a rough day. Don't need advice. Just need someone to know I'm not okay right now."

4. The Micro-Boundary

One small "no" per day. Build the muscle gradually.

- "I can't stay late today"

- "Let me think about that"

- "I need a minute"

THE SOCIAL MEDIA COMPARISON TRAP

Stop scrolling through other people's highlight reels when you're living in your outtakes.

Reality check: That colleague posting about their "amazing career opportunity" might be crying in their car too. That friend's "blessed family" posts don't show the 2 AM arguments about money.

Your new social media rule: If it makes you feel worse about your life, unfollow it. Your peace of mind is worth more than staying connected to someone's curated performance.

WHEN YOUR PARENTS DON'T UNDERSTAND

"In my day, we just worked hard and didn't complain."

Thanks, Mom. But in your day, one salary could buy a house, and therapy wasn't something you needed a GoFundMe for.

You don't need their permission to prioritize your mental health.

You don't need to explain why you can't work 80-hour weeks and still show up to every family gathering with a smile.

Your mental health is not a generational debate. It's a personal necessity.

THE MIDNIGHT CAREER CRISIS

It's 1 AM. You're wide awake, calculating how many years you have left until retirement. The math is depressing.

The question that haunts you: "Is this it? Is this all there is?"

Here's what I know: That question isn't a crisis. It's an invitation.

An invitation to stop sleepwalking through your one precious life.

The antidote to existential dread: One authentic choice per day. Stop asking "What should I do?" Start asking "What feels true?"

THE CHALLENGE

REBUILDING FROM THE GROUND UP

You've been surviving on fumes. Now it's time to build something sustainable.

Phase 1: Recognition

Daily question: "What part of my life feels most out of alignment?"

Don't fix it yet. Just notice it. Write it down. Stop pretending it's fine.

Phase 2: Small Rebellions

Weekly challenge: Do one thing that feels authentic but scary.

- Have that hard conversation
- Say no to something you don't want to do
- Ask for what you need
- Take a day off without justifying it

Phase 3: Structural Changes

Monthly focus: Change one big thing that's draining your soul.

- Job, relationship, living situation, commitments
- Not all at once. One at a time.
- With support. With a plan. But without apology.

THE NEW DEFINITION OF SUCCESS

Old definition: More money, bigger house, busier schedule, everyone else's approval.

New definition: I sleep well. I like the person I'm becoming. My relationships are real. My work matters to me. I'm not constantly exhausted.

The metric that matters: How often do you feel like yourself?

If the answer is "rarely," it's time to make some changes.

YOUR RESILIENCE MANIFESTO

Write this down. Tape it to your bathroom mirror. Make it your phone wallpaper:

"I will not shrink to make others comfortable. I will not set myself on fire to keep others warm. I will not apologize for taking up space. I will not abandon myself for anyone's approval. I am not broken. I am breaking free."

THE DAILY PRACTICE

Real resilience isn't built in dramatic moments. It's built in Tuesday afternoon decisions.

Every morning, ask yourself:

- How do I want to feel at the end of today?
- What's one thing I can do today that aligns with who I'm becoming?
- What boundary do I need to maintain today?

Every evening, check in:

- Did I abandon myself today or stay true?
- What felt authentic?
- What felt like performance?

WHAT HAPPENS NEXT

You close this chapter and go back to your life. But something's different now.

You have words for feelings you couldn't name before. You have permission to need what you need. You have tools for the moments when life gets sideways.

Most importantly: You have proof that you're not broken. You're not behind. You're not too late.

You're exactly where you need to be to start building something real.

The only person who can save your life is you.

The good news? You're more than capable.

The even better news? You don't have to do it alone.

YOUR NEXT MOVE

Don't just read this and move on. Do something with it.

Right now, text someone: "I'm reading this book about resilience and realized I've been abandoning myself to keep everyone else happy. Working on changing that."

This week, try one thing: Pick the smallest boundary you need to set. Practice it in the mirror. Then do it.

This month, get honest: What's the one area of your life that's most out of alignment? Write it down. Make a plan. Start changing it.

Your future self is counting on the decisions you make today.

Don't let them down.

You are not broken. You are becoming and that makes all the difference.

CHAPTER FOUR

PERMISSION TO BE DIFFERENT

"I'd rather be hated for who I am than loved for who I'm not."
Author Unknown

SOMEONE WHO FINALLY GOT TIRED OF THE BULLSHIT

You've burned the script.
You've started to design a life that fits.

Now comes the resistance.
Not from the world, but from within you.

Because as you change, something pulls at you.
A voice whispers, "Don't go too far."
"You can't afford to rock the boat."
"What if you lose what little security you have?"

That voice isn't your enemy.
It's your conditioning.

It's the ghost of every expectation you've ever tried to meet.
And every bill you're terrified you won't be able to pay.

And its weapon of choice is guilt.

THIS IS ABOUT RECLAIMING YOURSELF, EVEN WHEN YOU'RE BROKE

You weren't born to blend in.
You weren't born to serve someone else's vision or contort yourself to fit lives that never asked what you wanted.

But let's be real – you also weren't born with a trust fund.

This chapter is about permission. The kind you can give yourself even when:

- Your bank account says "no"

- Your family depends on your paycheck

- You're 35 with a mortgage and feel like it's too late

- You've got student loans that'll outlive you

- You're too exhausted from survival to think about dreams

Permission to:

- Leave what doesn't fit (even if you have to do it slowly)

- Speak what feels true (even if it makes people uncomfortable)

- Choose what aligns (within the constraints of real life)

- Disappoint people you love (because their comfort isn't worth your soul)

- Be a version of yourself others don't understand (even if they pay your bills)

Difference isn't disloyalty.
It's clarity.

And clarity is power, even when you're working two jobs to survive.

WHY YOU WERE TRAINED TO CONFORM (AND WHY IT'S KILLING YOU)

Let's go back.

From an early age, you were rewarded for fitting in.

- Sit still
- Don't speak unless spoken to
- Follow the rules
- Smile for the camera
- Don't rock the boat
- Be agreeable
- Get a "good job" with benefits
- Don't ask for too much

Color inside the lines, and you were praised.
Step outside, and you were labeled.

The child who questioned authority?
Disrespectful.
The one who felt deeply?
Too sensitive.
The one who refused to stay silent?
Problematic.
The one who wanted something different?
Unrealistic.

So you learned to shrink.

Psychologist Dr. Gabor Maté explains:

"Children will often choose attachment over authenticity, because survival depends on it."

You didn't betray yourself because you were weak.
You did it to survive.
In a system that rewarded sameness and punished difference, you learned the safest thing to be was invisible.

And now you're an adult, and that same system has you trapped in a cubicle, drowning in debt, wondering where the hell your life went.

Now it's time to unlearn that survival script, even if you have to do it while keeping your day job.

THE HIGH COST OF BLENDING IN (THAT NOBODY COUNTS)

What's the price of performing?

- Emotional numbness (but hey, at least you're "stable")

- Quiet resentment (that you swallow every Monday morning)

- A broken instinct (you don't even know what you want anymore)

- Relationships built on roles, not reality

- Years lost to paths that were never yours

- Sunday Scaries that make you physically sick

- The slow death of everything that made you feel alive

Worst of all?
You forget the sound of your own voice.

That's the tax conformity demands: your SELF.

And unlike your actual taxes, this one never gets you a refund.

YOUR DIFFERENCE IS NOT A LIABILITY (IT'S YOUR ONLY WAY OUT)

Here's the truth most systems never tell you:

What makes you different is what makes you dangerous, in the best way.

Your difference isn't a defect. It's your edge.
It's how you see.
How you move.
How you disrupt.
How you might actually escape the hamster wheel.

Look at the ones who changed culture, art, or the way we think:

- Maya Angelou (wrote her first book at 41)

- Colonel Sanders (started KFC at 62)

- Vera Wang (entered fashion at 40)

- Laura Ingalls Wilder (published her first book at 65)

- Samuel L. Jackson (didn't get famous until his 40s)

None of them got there by blending in.
Most of them got there later in life.
After they stopped giving a damn about fitting in.

They got there by protecting the very thing the world tried to erase.

They didn't succeed because they were acceptable.
They succeeded because they were undeniable.

You're not here to be a duplicate.
You're here to be unrepeatable.

Even if you're starting at 35. Even if you're broke. Even if you're scared shitless.

THE GUILT THAT COMES WITH GROWTH (WHEN YOU CAN'T AFFORD THERAPY)

Let's name what most people run from:
Guilt.

It shows up when you start to evolve.

- Guilt for wanting more (when you should be "grateful")

- Guilt for changing (when people depend on the old you)

- Guilt for saying "no" (when everyone needs something from you)

- Guilt for being "too much" (when you're supposed to be manageable)

- Guilt for outgrowing who you used to be (when that person paid the bills)

But guilt doesn't always mean wrong.
Sometimes, it just means different.

Growth violates the rules of the old script.
That's why guilt flares up.
It's not evidence of failure; it's proof of movement.

You're not betraying anyone by becoming who you are.
You're just no longer betraying yourself.

And if that makes people uncomfortable? Good. Maybe it's time they examined their own lives instead of policing yours.

THE PSYCHOLOGY OF PERMISSION (YOUR INTERNAL PRISON GUARD)

According to Dr. Kristin Neff, a pioneer in self-compassion research, the voice inside you that doubts and delays isn't evil. It's scared.

That inner critic was built for survival, not truth.

It's trying to protect you from rejection, from failure, from shame.

From losing the little security you have.

But in protecting you, it keeps you small.

It says:

- "Don't speak too loud; they'll think you're arrogant."

- "Don't quit that job; you need the insurance."

- "Don't be so emotional; it makes you unemployable."

- "Don't tell the truth; they'll replace you with someone easier."

- "Don't ask for more; you're lucky to have what you've got."

These aren't instructions.

They're fear in work clothes.

And here's the pivot –

You don't conquer that voice with violence.

You outgrow it, with clarity and compassion.

Say this out loud:

"I hear you. I know you're afraid. But staying small isn't keeping me safe anymore. It's slowly killing me. And I'm not that powerless child anymore."

That's not rebellion.

That's survival.

YOU'RE NOT SELFISH. YOU'RE FINALLY AWAKE

Let's burn a lie that's been passed down like gospel.

Choosing yourself is not selfish.

It's intelligent.
It's necessary.
It's overdue.

Selfishness is harming others to get ahead.
Self-awareness is refusing to harm yourself to keep the peace.

Big difference.

You can't keep dimming your light to protect other peoples' insecurities.

That's not humility.
That's self-abandonment in slow motion.

Every time you say yes when you mean no, you don't just lie – you disappear.

And here's the kicker: Your misery isn't helping anyone. Your kids don't need a martyr; they need a model. Your partner doesn't need your resentment; they need your honesty. Your employer doesn't deserve your soul; they pay for your time.

WHAT THEY REALLY MEAN WHEN THEY SAY "YOU'VE CHANGED"

You'll hear it.

- "You've changed."

- "You're not like you used to be."

- "What happened to the old you?"

- "You've become difficult."

- "You used to be so easy-going."

Here's the translation:

"You stopped doing what made me comfortable."
"You're no longer convenient for my needs."
"I miss being able to take you for granted."

Growth threatens anyone who benefited from your compliance.

But this isn't their story. It's yours.

And the "old you" they miss?
That version wasn't real. It was edited for their comfort, not your truth.

THE SINGLE MOM WHO STOPPED APOLOGIZING

Maria, 34. Two kids. Working at a call center by day, cleaning offices at night. Exhausted. Broke. Invisible.

She'd been the "good girl" her whole life. Never complained. Always said yes. Kept everyone happy while slowly disappearing.

Then her 8-year-old daughter asked her: "Mommy, why do you always say sorry?"

That broke something open.

Maria realized she apologized for everything:

*Taking space in the break room

*Asking for her paycheck on time

*Needing to leave when her shift ended

*Having opinions

*Existing

The next day, she walked into her supervisor's office and said something she'd never said before.

"I need to talk about my schedule."

Not "Sorry to bother you, but..."
Not "I hate to ask, but..."
Just: "I need to talk."

She negotiated better hours. Asked for a raise. Got it.

Six months later, she left the call center for a better job. Then another one.

Maria didn't become a CEO overnight. She didn't write a bestseller or start a viral TikTok.

She just stopped apologizing for taking up space in her own life.

That's revolution enough.

THE WORKING-CLASS TRUTH ABOUT CHANGE

Let's get real about something the self-help industry won't tell you.

Most advice about "following your passion" comes from people who never had to choose between their dreams and their kids' dinner.

"Just quit your job and pursue your purpose!" says someone whose daddy paid for their startup.

"Money isn't everything!" says someone who's never been broke.

"Do what you love!" says someone who's never worked a soul-crushing job to keep the lights on.

Here's the working-class truth about change–

You don't have to blow up your life to reclaim it.

You can:

- Start saying no to overtime that's killing your spirit

- Stop pretending to agree with your boss's terrible ideas

- Use your lunch break to sketch, write, or dream instead of scrolling

- Apply for better jobs on your own timeline

- Save money (even $20 a month) toward something that matters to you

- Tell your family what you actually think instead of what keeps the peace

- Wear something that makes you feel alive, even to your dead-end job

- Stop apologizing for having needs, opinions, and boundaries

Change doesn't have to be dramatic to be real.

Sometimes the most radical thing you can do is stop shrinking.

> **THE CHALLENGE**

GET TO KNOW THESE TOOLS

Tool: The "Stealth Revolution" Practice

Can't afford to make big moves right now? Start small. Start secret. Start today.

Step 1: Stop Apologizing

- Don't say "sorry" unless you actually did something wrong

- Replace "Sorry to bother you" with "Quick question"

- Replace "Sorry I'm late" with "Thanks for waiting"

- Notice how often you apologize for existing

Step 2: Claim Your Space

- Sit up straighter in meetings

- Don't make yourself smaller when others enter a room

- Take up your fair share of conversation

- Stop prefacing your ideas with "This might be stupid, but..."

Step 3: Practice the Truth

- When someone asks how you are, give a real answer (not always "fine")

- Share one honest opinion per day

- Say "I don't know" instead of pretending you do

- Stop laughing at jokes that aren't funny

Step 4: Protect Your Energy

- Say no to one thing you don't want to do

- Leave conversations and relationships that drain you

- Stop checking your phone first thing in the morning

- Go to bed when you're tired, not when you think you should

This isn't therapy. It's training.

Training yourself to remember. You have a right to exist fully.

THE WAREHOUSE WORKER WHO BECAME AN ARTIST (WITHOUT QUITTING HIS DAY JOB)

James worked third shift at Amazon. 50 hours a week. Body breaking down. Soul already dead.

But James had a secret: He drew. In the break room. On napkins. Sketches of his coworkers, the machinery, the exhaustion on everyone's faces.

One day, a coworker saw his sketches and said, "Damn, man. You're good. You should do something with this." James laughed it off. "Yeah, right. I'm 42. I'm not going to art school."

But the comment stuck.

James started small:

*Drew for 30 minutes before his shift

*Posted his sketches on Instagram (gained 50 followers)

*Sold his first drawing for $20 (to a coworker)

*Used that $20 to buy better pens

Two years later, James is still at Amazon. But now he makes an extra $500 a month selling art. More importantly, he has hope. He's planning his exit. Slowly. Carefully. But with purpose.

James didn't follow his passion recklessly. He followed it strategically. That's how real people change real lives.

Tool: The "Wrong Room" Filter

If you often feel:

- Like you're too much

- Like you have to dumb yourself down

- Like your dreams are "unrealistic"

- Like your ideas get blank stares

- Like your boundaries are met with guilt trips

- Like you're crazy for wanting more

You're not broken.
You're just in the wrong room.

Here's your filter. Ask yourself:

- Do I feel more energized or drained around these people?

- Do they celebrate truth, or only comfort?

- Do they hold space for who I'm becoming, or just who I used to be?

- When I share good news, are they genuinely happy for me?

- Do they support my growth or try to keep me small?

Sometimes, the most powerful thing you can do is leave the table you've been begging to sit at.

You're not difficult.
You're evolving.

And evolution is always uncomfortable for the people who want you to stay the same.

THE RAGE YOU'RE NOT ALLOWED TO FEEL

Let's talk about the anger.

The white-hot rage at realizing you've wasted years being who other people needed you to be.

The fury at all the times you said yes when you meant no.

The resentment toward everyone who benefited from your silence.

The grief for the person you might have been if you'd had permission to be yourself from the beginning.

That anger? IT'S VALID.

You have every right to be pissed.

At the system that taught you to shrink.
At the people who took advantage of your compliance.
At yourself for playing along for so long.

Feel it. All of it.

But don't get stuck there.

Use that rage as fuel. Let it burn away everything that isn't really you.

Your anger isn't a character flaw; it's information.
It's your soul saying "Never again."

PERMISSION MAP: FOUR PLACES YOU MUST RECLAIM (STARTING NOW)

This part is practical. Tactical. Clear.

Here are four places where you need to give yourself full permission (no apology, no delay):

1. Permission to Speak

Say the thing. Even if your voice shakes.

- Say "No."
- Say "I need space."

- Say "This isn't working."

- Say "I want more."

- Say "I don't agree."

- Say "I'm not okay."

- Say "That's not my job."

- Say "I can't work late tonight."

Silence isn't strength when it's rooted in fear.

2. Permission to Take Up Space

You're allowed to be visible.
To express yourself.
To not apologize for existing.

Stop shrinking in rooms you're qualified to lead in.

3. Permission to Walk Away

Not everything deserves your loyalty.
Not every connection is meant to last.
Not every job is worth your mental health.

Quitting isn't weakness. Staying in what kills you is.

4. Permission to Be Seen Fully

You don't have to edit your truth for approval.

- Your weirdness? Valuable.

- Your backstory? Sacred.

- Your honesty? Liberating.

- Your struggles? Relatable.

- Your dreams? Valid, even if they seem impossible.

The right people don't need the filtered version of you. They need the real one.

THE 30-YEAR-OLD TRUTH NOBODY TELLS YOU

If you're reading this in your 30s or 40s, you've probably thought:

"It's too late. I missed my chance. I should have figured this out by 25."

That's bullshit.

Most people don't even know who they are until their 30s.
Most people spend their 20s trying to become who they think they should be.
Most people don't have the guts to change until life forces them to.

Your 30s aren't when life ends; they're when it begins.

Because by 30, you've usually:

- Made enough mistakes to know what doesn't work

- Built enough skills to actually do something about it

- Gotten tired enough of pretending to finally choose authenticity

- Realized that "someday" isn't coming. You have to create it

Starting over at 30 isn't late. It's right on time.

Tool: The "Not This" Inventory

Still unsure who you are?
Start with what you're *not*.

Clarity doesn't always begin with revelation.
Sometimes, it begins with subtraction.

Take out a sheet of paper.
Write 20 sentences starting with:

"I'm not someone who..."

Examples:

- "I'm not someone who pretends to agree to keep the peace."
- "I'm not someone who stays silent when something needs to be said."
- "I'm not someone who works 60 hours a week just to impress people I don't like."
- "I'm not someone who waits to be chosen."
- "I'm not someone who apologizes for having needs."
- "I'm not someone who accepts less than I deserve because I'm afraid to ask for more."

This is spiritual excavation.
Every false identity you let go of creates space for the real one to emerge.

This isn't fluff.
It's recovery.
It's how you unlearn who the world told you to be and remember who you actually are.

THE ECONOMICS OF AUTHENTICITY

Here's what they don't tell you about being yourself:

It might cost you some things short-term.
But it pays dividends long-term.

When you stop pretending:

- You attract better opportunities (because you're not hiding your strengths)
- You build real relationships (because people can actually see you)

- You make better decisions (because you know what you actually want)

- You waste less time and energy (because you're not maintaining a fake persona)

- You become irreplaceable (because authentic people are rare)

Authenticity isn't just morally right; it's economically smart.

The job market rewards people who know who they are.
The dating market rewards people who aren't pretending.
The friendship market rewards people who tell the truth.

Being fake is expensive. Being real is an investment.

"YOU WERE ALWAYS TOO MUCH"

Ana always heard the same things growing up: "You're too emotional. You ask too many questions. You care too much. You want too much. Calm down. Don't be so intense."

She believed it.
She dimmed her voice in school.
Softened her ambition at work.
Played small in relationships.
Made herself digestible.

By thirty, Ana had become a ghost - present, functional, polite... and empty.

She worked in HR at a mid-sized company. Made decent money. Had a nice apartment. Should have been grateful.

Instead, she cried in her car after work every day.

Then, at a leadership retreat her company paid for, someone looked her dead in the eye and said:

"You're not too much. You were just in the wrong rooms."

That broke her and rebuilt her.

Ana didn't quit her job the next day. She couldn't afford to.

But she stopped apologizing.
She started speaking up in meetings.
She applied for a role in employee advocacy.
She started a company newsletter highlighting worker concerns.

Two years later, Ana runs employee relations for a tech startup. She makes twice what she used to. More importantly, she uses her "too much" energy to fight for people who don't have a voice.

The thing that made her "difficult" became her superpower.

Not because she changed herself.
Because she finally stopped hiding.

LET THEM MISUNDERSTAND YOU (IT'S NOT YOUR JOB TO EXPLAIN)

This is the part most people avoid.

We're trained to explain ourselves.
To soften the truth.
To make our choices more digestible.
To filter our pain into something presentable.

But here's the truth:
If the truth is filtered, it's no longer the truth.

Let them misunderstand you.

Let them:

- Wonder why you're quieter now

- Think you're arrogant for setting boundaries

- Be confused when you no longer chase what used to drain you

- Sit with your silence instead of your explanation

- Miss the version of you that was easier to manage

You are not here to be decoded.
You are not a product with an instruction manual.
You are a person.

And if someone can only love the edited version of you, they don't love you.
They love their comfort.

You don't owe anyone a performance, especially not the ones who benefited from your silence.

Let them talk.
Let them assume.
Let them miss the version of you that was easy to manage.

You're not here to be manageable.
You're here to be whole.

THE GENERATIONAL WEIGHT (FOR THOSE CARRYING FAMILY EXPECTATIONS)

Some of you aren't just navigating personal change.
You're carrying generations of expectation.

- You might be the first to challenge traditions that kept your family afloat

- You might be the first to say, "This ends with me"

- You might be living a life no one in your bloodline has modeled

- You might be disappointing people who sacrificed for you to have "opportunities" they never had

That isn't a small thing.
That's revolutionary work.

And revolutions don't come with applause.

You will be misunderstood.
You will carry guilt.
You will be called selfish, ungrateful, "too good" for where you came from.

But you might also become the one your great-grandchildren point to and say:

"That's where it all started. That's when our family learned we had choices."

Tool: The Ancestral Permission Letter

Write this. You don't have to send it. But you have to mean it.

"I honor what you gave me. I see what you endured.
I cannot continue the patterns that broke you.
I am not rejecting you; I am healing us both.
I give myself permission to want more than survival.
I give myself permission to dream beyond fear.
And I give the next generation something different:
Truth. Freedom. Permission to be themselves."

Sometimes the permission you need isn't from your boss or your partner.
It's from your past.

Sometimes you're not just liberating yourself; you're freeing centuries of silence.

THE TRUTH ABOUT BELONGING VS. FITTING IN

Let's set the record straight:

Fitting in is when you *change* yourself to be accepted.
Belonging is when you're accepted *because* you didn't.

One is performance.
The other is connection.

Researcher Brené Brown puts it this way:

"True belonging doesn't require you to change who you are; it requires you to be who you are."

But most people confuse the two.
They chase approval and call it safety.

So they mold themselves (shrink themselves) into the kind of person who will be liked.
And in doing so, they vanish.

Here's the irony:
You can be surrounded by people and still feel completely alone, because they only know the version of you you've packaged for their comfort.

Belonging begins with self-belonging.

You cannot ask others to accept you until you've accepted yourself.

YOUR NEW OPERATING SYSTEM

Write this. Say it. Repeat it.

I no longer owe anyone the version of me they invented.
I don't exist to be digestible, manageable, or predictable.
I am allowed to change, even if others don't understand.
I choose truth over performance.
I give myself full permission to be different.
If it costs me my truth, it's too expensive.

Say it again tomorrow.
And again the day after.

Make it your new operating system.

FINAL TRUTH: YOU WERE NEVER MEANT TO BE AVERAGE

You weren't born to blend into a bland, forgettable life.

You weren't built to color inside someone else's lines.

You weren't created to live on autopilot, saying what's safe, doing what's expected, pretending it's enough.

You were born for:

- Depth
- Meaning
- Truth
- Fire
- Your own damn life

And getting there requires one thing above all.
The courage to be different.

Not as rebellion.
As design.

CLOSING WORDS: THE PRICE AND THE REWARD

You will lose things as you become more yourself.
Not maybe. Not if. You will.

You'll lose:

- People who only liked the edited version
- Opportunities that required you to shrink
- Illusions that kept you stuck
- Comforts that were quietly killing you
- The safety of being invisible

But in their place, you'll gain what can't be faked:

- Peace that isn't performative
- Power rooted in truth
- Relationships built on honesty, not compliance
- Creative freedom (even if you express it in small ways)
- Joy that doesn't come with a mask
- A life that finally feels like yours
- The ability to look in the mirror without flinching

So here's your new line to live by: **"If it costs me my truth, it's too expensive."**

You don't need anyone to stamp that permission slip for you. You already signed it when you chose this book, this chapter, this path.

Now live accordingly.

Even if you have to do it slowly.
Even if you have to do it scared.
Even if you have to do it while keeping your day job.

Your difference isn't the obstacle; it's the foundation. Build from there.

CHAPTER FIVE

REAL CONFIDENCE COMES FROM CONSEQUENCE

"You get confidence not from shouting affirmations in the mirror but from having a stack of undeniable proof that you are who you say you are."
Alex Hormozi

THE LIE THEY SOLD YOU

They told you confidence was a mindset. That you just needed to think bigger. Speak louder. "Act like you own the room." More bullshit.

Here's what they didn't tell you. You're not lacking confidence because you don't believe in yourself enough. You're lacking confidence because you've spent the last decade making promises to yourself that you never kept. Every time you hit snooze instead of going to the gym. Every time you said "next Monday" instead of today. Every time you swallowed your words in that meeting because speaking up felt too risky.

Your subconscious is keeping score. And right now, you're losing.

Confidence isn't a costume you throw on. It's a scar. It's proof that you've done hard things when it mattered. It's the muscle memory of showing up when every fiber of your being wanted to hide.

WHY YOU REALLY FEEL STUCK

Let me guess your Sunday nights. That sick feeling in your stomach knowing Monday's coming. Another week of pretending your job matters. Another week of being the "responsible one" while watching everyone else take risks you're too scared to take.

You've got golden handcuffs, and you know it. The mortgage, the car payments, the expectations. You're trapped by a lifestyle you built to impress people you don't even like. And the worst part? You're angry at yourself for wanting more when you "should be grateful."

Here's the truth nobody wants to say: You're not ungrateful. You're dying inside. There's a version of you that exists in some parallel universe who took the risks, made the moves, and is living the life you think about at 2 AM when you can't sleep.

That version of you has confidence. Not because they're special. Because they have receipts.

STOP ASKING FOR CONFIDENCE. CREATE CONSEQUENCES.

The man who walks into a room and commands respect without saying a word? He's not naturally confident. He's battle-tested.

He's the guy who:

- Applied for the job requiring 5 years experience when he had 3 (He got it!)

- Left the toxic workplace without another job lined up (He survived)

- Had the conversation with his wife about their dead bedroom (He saved his marriage)

- Told his parents he wasn't coming to Christmas because they treat him like shit (He stopped being their emotional punching bag)

Every time he acted when he was afraid, he built proof. Not for others. For himself.

You want to feel more solid? Stop fantasizing about the perfect moment and start choosing harder conversations.

Tell your boss you deserve the promotion instead of hoping he notices. Say no to your friend who only calls when she needs something. Apply for the job that scares you instead of the one you're "qualified" for. Book the trip instead of talking about it for another year.

THE PSYCHOLOGY OF CONSEQUENCE: WHY YOUR BRAIN DOESN'T TRUST YOU

Your brain doesn't care what you say. It watches what you do.

Every time you choose Netflix over the gym, your brain learns: "We don't follow through." Every time you avoid the difficult conversation, your brain learns: "We fold under pressure." Every time you pick safe over scary, your brain learns: "We're not built for risk."

But here's the flip side: Every time you do the thing that makes you uncomfortable, your brain learns: "We can handle hard things." Every time you speak up when your voice shakes, your brain learns: "We don't back down." Every time you choose growth over comfort, your brain learns: "We're dangerous."

Confidence is pattern recognition. Your mental health is watching. The scoreboard doesn't lie.

The gap between what you say you'll do and what you actually prove you can do? That's your confidence level.

Close the gap. You'll stop needing hype. You'll have receipts.

THE PERMISSION YOU'VE BEEN WAITING FOR

Here's what no one tells you: You don't need anyone's permission to disappoint them.

You don't need your parents' approval to change careers at 35. You don't need your spouse's excitement about your dreams. You don't need your friends to understand why you're not available every weekend anymore.

The people who love the old version of you will resist the new one. Not because they hate you. Because change is scary, and your growth reminds them of their stagnation.

Some relationships won't survive your evolution. That's not a bug; it's a feature.

FAIL FORWARD (THE DETROIT GYM STORY)

There's a man in Detroit I know. Late 40s. Steel-gray beard. Divorced. Every morning, he's in the gym before sunrise.

His wife left him two years ago. Said he'd "given up on life." She wasn't wrong. Dead-end job, dad bod, zero ambition. He was sleepwalking through his existence.

The divorce papers were his wake-up call.

Now? Same hoodie. Same silence. Same 5 AM consistency. No Instagram. No before-and-after photos. Just a man rebuilding himself one rep at a time.

One morning, a kid asks him: "Why are you here this early if no one's watching?"

The man pauses mid-rep: *"I'm not training for attention. I'm training so the next time life tries to break me, I'm ready."*

Six months later, he got promoted. Not because he asked for it. Because he'd become the kind of man who deserved it.

That's confidence. Not the kind that needs validation. The kind that can handle whatever comes next.

THE CHALLENGE

THE NO-BULLSHIT ACTION PLAN

Want to build real confidence? Here's your homework:

Step 1: Have one difficult conversation you've been avoiding. Your boss about a raise. Your partner about the thing that's bothering you. Your parents about their guilt trips.

Step 2: Do something that scares you professionally. Apply for the stretch role. Pitch the idea. Start the side business.

Step 3: Say no to something you always say yes to. The family obligation that drains you. The friend who takes advantage. The commitment you hate.

Step 4: Invest in yourself in a way that makes you uncomfortable. The course that costs more than you want to spend. The coach you can't quite afford. The gym membership you'll actually use.

No excuses. No "when I'm ready." Ready is a myth. Scared and moving forward? That's courage.

THE PERSON YOU'RE BECOMING

Six months from now, there's a version of you walking around with fire behind their eyes.

They've had the hard conversations. They've made the scary moves. They've disappointed some people and found peace with it.

Their confidence isn't loud; it's lethal.

Not because they talk about it, but because they walk with the quiet power of someone who's kept promises to themselves when no one was watching.

They don't perform. They decide. They don't chase approval. They create value. They don't wait for permission. They give it to themselves.

THE FINAL QUESTION

"If the applause stopped tomorrow, would you still show up the same way?"

Most people won't answer that honestly. Because they know what silence would reveal about their motivation.

But you're not most people anymore.

You're building the kind of self that nothing (not failure, not rejection, not loss) can shake. Because you've got proof. Not proof for them. Proof for you.

The next version of you is watching. What will you have to show?

Now stop reading. Start moving. The confidence you want is on the other side of the conversation you're avoiding.

CHAPTER SIX

THE SELF-MADE CAGE

"What protected you then is poisoning you now. The armor became a cage, and survival became the prison."
Author Unknown

THE PRISON YOU BUILT TO SURVIVE

You didn't fail at life. You got good at surviving it. And now that skill is killing you.

You didn't choose the prison. You built it. Brick by brick. Out of fear. Out of pain. Out of survival.

And at the time, it made sense.

You needed a way to feel safe. To stay small enough not to be a threat. To be useful enough not to be discarded. To be strong enough not to break.

So you got quiet. Or funny. Or productive. Or angry. Or invisible.

Whatever it took to stay alive, you did it.

And it worked.

That's the dangerous part.

SURVIVAL HAS A COST

The walls you built back then still surround you now.

But now, they don't protect you. They isolate you. They suffocate you. They steal connection, joy, and breath.

You sit in your car after work, too exhausted to go inside and pretend you're okay. You refresh your bank balance, hoping the number has changed, knowing it hasn't. Sunday night hits and your chest tightens because Monday means another week of going through the motions.

Survival made you sharp. It made you alert. It made you resilient.

But it also made you afraid of your freedom, because freedom requires feeling again and risking again. Choosing without guarantees. And that's terrifying when you've spent years making sure nothing could hurt you.

EVERYONE BUILDS THEIR VERSION

Some build with silence. Some with charm. Some with success. Some with control. Some with Netflix and takeout. Some stay so busy they never have to think.

The material doesn't matter. What matters is that it traps you.

And what traps you isn't the world. It's the script you've rehearsed so often it became identity:

• "I don't need anyone." • "I'm fine." • "If I speak up, I'll lose them." • "If I slow down, I'll collapse." • "If I ask for help, I'm weak." • "If they knew me, they'd leave." • "This is just how life is."

That's not personality. That's a defense mechanism for making an impression of who you think you should be.

You're not broken. You're overprotected.

THE CORPORATE CAGE

Sara was the one everyone could count on. Senior project manager. Early 30s. $127,000 salary that looked good on paper but felt like prison wages when you factor in the $2,400 mortgage, $89,000 in student loans, and the fact that she hadn't taken a real vacation in three years.

She was the one who answered emails at 11:47 PM and fixed disasters before the morning coffee finished brewing. Her team called her "unshakeable." Her friends called her "lucky to have such a stable job."

What they didn't see– the Sunday night panic attacks. The commute fantasies about driving past her exit and never coming back. The way she'd sit in her car after work, too drained to walk to her front door.

She didn't cry. She didn't cancel. She didn't complain. She just slowly disappeared inside her own life.

Every week looked identical: color-coded calendars that felt like handcuffs, PowerPoint decks that made her soul die a little more, polite nods while screaming inside. The chest tightness that started as "stress" became her baseline. She couldn't remember what relaxed felt like.

But here's the thing everyone missed: Sara wasn't fine. She was fucking numb.

One Thursday, during a team Zoom call, someone cracked a joke and everyone laughed. Sara laughed too not because it was funny, but because that's what the reliable, likable leader was supposed to do. After the call, she shut her laptop and sat in the silence of her apartment. For the first time in months, she noticed the weight crushing her chest.

And for the first time in years, she heard her voice whisper: *"I can't do this anymore."*

That night, she did something she hadn't done in four years. She called in sick. Not because she had a fever. Because she was exhausted from being a role instead of a person. Because she was tired of being everyone's backup plan while having no plan for herself.

That wasn't quitting. That was the first crack in the wall.

YOU DIDN'T HEAL. YOU ADAPTED.

Most people don't heal. They just reorganize around the pain.

You got smarter. You got more efficient. More competent. But also colder. More distant. Less tolerant of softness (even your own).

You call it strength. But it's just endurance in disguise.

And endurance is noble when the war is active. But when the war is over, it turns your life into a permanent battlefield where Tuesday at 3pm feels like a small death.

THE BOY WHO NEVER CRIED

Jamal learned early that feelings were fucking dangerous.

His father called emotions "drama." His mother called crying "a waste of time that won't pay bills." By 10, he stopped asking for hugs. By 14, he got the "man up" speech so many times he could recite it. By 28, he was the guy who fixed everything—cars, bills, broken relationships, family crises—but never his shit.

He didn't break. He just went numb.

Everyone called him "strong." Women dated him because he was "stable." Friends dumped their problems on him because he "could handle it." What they didn't know: he couldn't feel anything anymore. Joy, sadness, anger—it all felt like static.

At his childhood best friend's funeral, he stood by the casket watching everyone else weep. He felt... nothing. Not because he didn't care. Because twenty years of swallowing his feelings had turned him into an emotional zombie.

That night, he sat in his car in the funeral home parking lot. Just sat there. Until something inside him finally cracked. The first tear fell. Then another. Then twenty years of swallowed rage, grief, and exhaustion erupted from his chest like a dam bursting.

No one saw it. No one needed to. But that moment of ugly crying in a Honda Civic at 3 AM was the beginning of feeling human again.

THE ARMOR BECAME A CAGE

You wore armor to survive.

It kept the chaos out. It numbed the fear. It let you walk through hell without flinching.

But armor doesn't discriminate. It blocks joy as well as pain. Truth as well as lies. Love as well as harm.

You can't feel anything deeply with armor on; not even yourself.

You look in the mirror and don't see a person. You see a role. A function. A version you never chose but learned to play too well.

And now? You're alone inside your skin, scrolling your phone at 3 am wondering if this is all there is.

YOUR STRENGTH ISN'T A GIFT. IT'S A STORY YOU WROTE TO SURVIVE.

Nobody comes through clean.

But some of us dress survival in noble terms: Responsibility. Independence. Maturity. Being "low-maintenance."

We make it sound like a strength. But underneath that control is someone who was never allowed to need. Someone who had to hold it together when everything was falling apart. Someone who became reliable because no one else was.

They never disappeared. They just went quiet.

Now you call it resilience. But it's just that scared part of you whispering, "Can I stop now?"

REST ISN'T WEAKNESS. IT'S PERMISSION.

If you've carried the load for years (the family, the bills, the expectations, the silence), then the rest will feel like failure.

Stillness will feel like danger because stillness is where the thoughts catch up. Where you remember who you used to be before you became who you had to be.

But here's the truth: When pain catches up, it can finally be released.

It can breathe. It can soften. It can stop running your life from the shadows.

But only if you're willing to stop performing the version of you that can't feel.

WHAT PROTECTED YOU THEN IS POISONING YOU NOW

The mindset that once saved you? It's slowly destroying any chance of growth.

- Hyper-independence looks strong. But it kills intimacy.
- Control looks responsible. But it kills the part of you that used to dream.
- Staying busy looks productive. But it's just costly procrastination.
- "I'm fine" looks stable. But it breeds disease.

Your survival strategy became your sabotage.

And the more it worked, the harder it became to recognize. Because dysfunction that produces results gets rewarded. And you mistook applause for alignment.

But deep down, you knew. You weren't free. You were just needed.

YOU BECAME INDISPENSABLE SO YOU WOULDN'T BE LEFT

You over-delivered. Overcommitted. Or maybe you just showed up when others didn't. You became the one who handles it. The one who doesn't complain. The one who can take it.

Why?

Because if they needed you, they wouldn't abandon you. If they depended on you, they wouldn't notice how tired you were. If you kept fixing everything, no one would realize you were breaking.

That's not strength. That's fear. Camouflaged as reliability.

You became the person who handles it all. But no one checks on that person.

Because they think you don't break.

And the scariest part? You believed it too.

Until you didn't.

BREAKING DOESN'T ANNOUNCE ITSELF

It doesn't explode. It erodes.

- You wake up already tired.
- You say "I'm fine" automatically, even to yourself.
- You scroll to escape your thoughts.
- You can't cry, even when you want to.
- You avoid looking too long in mirrors.
- You feel nothing when good things happen.

That's not peace. That's prison.

And it's not sustainable.

If you won't let the mask crack, the person underneath will.

THE REALITY CHECK: WHY YOU FEEL LIKE SHIT

Before we get to the challenge, let's address the elephant in the room. Your life might suck right now. And that's not a mindset problem, that's a reality problem.

- You're not broken because you can't "manifest" your way out of student loans.
- You're not weak because positive thinking doesn't cure a toxic boss.
- You're not failing because you can't Instagram-quote your way out of genuine exhaustion.

Some situations are objectively terrible. Some jobs are soul-crushing. Some relationships are toxic. Some financial pressures are suffocating.

Stop trying to gratitude-journal your way out of legitimate problems.

3 SIGNS YOU'RE LIVING SOMEONE ELSE'S LIFE

1. You can't remember the last time you said "no" without guilt
2. Your weekends are spent recovering from your weeks, not living
3. You're more worried about disappointing others than disappointing yourself

FREEDOM ISN'T GIVEN. IT'S CHOSEN.

No one permits you to be human.

You don't earn healing with more performance.

You don't talk your way out of the cage. You stop reinforcing it.

- You stop apologizing for having needs.
- You stop proving your worth through exhaustion.
- You stop shrinking to stay palatable.
- You stop bleeding just to keep the peace.

That's not rebellion. That's recovery.

And it will feel wrong at first. Because trauma disguises healing as risk.

But you're not losing anything. You're remembering who you were before the fear took over.

THE WORK IS UNLEARNING

You don't need to become someone new. You need to unlearn the version you became to survive.

Unlearn the silence. Unlearn the shame. Unlearn the need to be useful in order to be loved.

And underneath? You'll find a version of you that's been waiting.

Not for success. Not for perfection. Just for permission.

HEALING REQUIRES GRIEF

Here's what no one tells you: Healing isn't just joy. It's grief.

Grief for the years you lost performing. Grief for the childhood you had to parent yourself through. Grief for the dreams you shelved because "be realistic." Grief for the person you never got to be, because survival came first.

You don't heal by ignoring the pain. You heal by facing it and mourning what you never received.

Only then can you release it. Only then can you choose, without dragging the past into every new beginning.

GET RID OF THAT SCRIPT

You were given a role.

Maybe it was The Provider. The Reliable One. The One Who Never Complains.

The One Who Has It Together. The One Who Doesn't Need Much.

And you played it well. Too well.

But that script is killing you.

It asks you to be a character instead of a person. To perform instead of live. To tolerate instead of transform.

Burn it.

You don't owe anyone the version of you that never got to choose.

THE CHALLENGE: THE UNFUCKING RITUAL

You've performed long enough. This week, you're going to stop being everyone's reliable backup plan and start being your own person.

Day 1: Name Your Prison

Write down 3 beliefs that are keeping you trapped:

- "I can't disappoint people"
- "If I slow down, everything will fall apart"
- "If they knew the real me, they'd leave"
- "I have to earn my worth through exhaustion"

Next to each, write where you learned it. Then ask: Is this true, or is this just fear wearing a business suit?

Day 2: Cancel Something

Cancel one obligation you agreed to out of guilt, not desire. When they ask why, say "I don't want to." Don't elaborate. Don't apologize. Don't give them a reason to argue with.

Watch them lose their shit when you stop being their reliable backup plan. That's not your problem anymore.

Day 3: Tell Someone the Truth

Tell one person how you're doing. Not "fine." Not "busy." Not "hanging in there." The unedited, unfiltered version.

"I'm drowning and pretending I'm swimming." "I hate my job but I'm scared to leave." "I'm lonely as hell but too tired to fix it."

Day 4: Do Something Unproductive

Take a nap. Watch a sad movie. Sit in your car and stare at nothing. Let yourself feel like shit without trying to fix it, optimize it, or turn it into a learning experience.

You don't have to be grateful for your struggles. You don't have to find the lesson. Sometimes life just sucks, and that's allowed.

Day 5: Write Your Permission Slip

Write yourself permission to be human and stick it somewhere you'll see it:

- "I no longer need to earn rest with exhaustion"
- "I'm allowed to want things"
- "Other people's disappointment is not my emergency"
- "I don't owe anyone my misery"

BUILD WHAT FEELS LIKE FREEDOM

Once you burn the script, you're left with something rare: Choice.

- Choose rest without guilt.
- Choose honesty over harmony.
- Choose feeling over functioning.
- Choose to be real over being right.

And if you don't know what feels like freedom? Start with this:

What feels like *you*?

Not the version they trained. Not the version they praised. Not the version you performed to survive.

But the version who breathes fully, loves openly, and sleeps deeply.

You're not gone. You're just buried under years of pretending.

YOU DON'T NEED TO DESERVE REST. YOU NEED TO RECLAIM IT.

You've spent years earning the right to pause. Stop earning it. Claim it.

You don't owe anyone exhaustion as proof of your loyalty. You don't have to be bleeding to be worthy of care. And you don't need another breakdown to justify asking for help.

Let this be the moment where rest becomes your rebellion. Where honesty becomes your strategy. Where wholeness becomes your goal.

THE HARD TRUTH

You don't heal by performing. You don't fix yourself by being perfect. You don't earn love by being useful.

You heal by stopping. By feeling. By admitting that the person you've been pretending to be is killing the person you are.

This week, stop rehearsing your role in everyone else's life. Start remembering you have your own.

The world will survive without your constant availability.

You might not survive with it.

FINAL THOUGHT: THE DOOR WAS NEVER LOCKED

This is the part they never told you. The prison wasn't locked. It never was.

You just forgot you had the key.

And the key is TRUTH. Raw. Personal. Inconvenient.

But once spoken, it cracks the walls. The same door in is the same door out.

You're not weak for being tired. You're not broken for needing more. You're not selfish for choosing to feel again.

You are ready.

To stop surviving. To start living. To finally, *finally*, walk free.

CHAPTER SEVEN

BUILDING UNSHAKABLE SELF-BELIEF

The Foundation of Every Bold Move (Even When You're Too Tired for Bold)

THE SUNDAY NIGHT REALITY CHECK

It's 9 PM on Sunday. Tomorrow is Monday. Again.

You're lying in bed doing the math. 47 more years until retirement. 47 years of pretending you give a shit about quarterly reports while your real life happens in the margins. Stolen moments between meetings. Weekend hours that feel too short. Vacation days you're afraid to take.

You tell people you're "fine" while secretly googling "is it too late to change careers at 34" during lunch breaks.

Here's what nobody talks about: The problem isn't that you lack ambition. The problem is that you've been grinding so hard just to keep up that you've forgotten you're allowed to want more.

Self-belief isn't about positive thinking your way out of real problems. It's about trusting yourself to navigate the mess, even when you're starting from exhausted, broke, or behind.

WHAT SELF-BELIEF ACTUALLY IS (NOT THE INSTAGRAM VERSION)

Self-Belief vs. Self-Esteem: The Difference That Changes Everything

Self-esteem = "I'm a good person"
Self-belief = "I can figure this out"

Here's why this matters: You can hate your current situation and still trust your ability to change it. You can feel like a failure at 35 and still believe you're capable of course-correcting.

Self-belief isn't feeling confident. It's acting anyway.

THE IMPOSTOR SYNDROME REALITY CHECK

Maya Angelou felt like a fraud. So did Tom Hanks. Michelle Obama still questions if she belongs in the room.

If you feel like everyone else has it figured out while you're barely holding it together, welcome to being human. The difference between people who move forward and people who stay stuck isn't confidence– it's the willingness to feel like an impostor and show up anyway.

Truth bomb: Everyone is making it up as they go along. Some people are just better at hiding it.

WHERE SELF-DOUBT REALLY COMES FROM (SPOILER: IT'S NOT YOUR FAULT)

THE CHILDHOOD PROGRAMMING THAT'S STILL RUNNING YOUR LIFE

If you grew up hearing:

- "Don't get your hopes up"
- "Money doesn't grow on trees"
- "Who do you think you are?"
- "Be grateful for what you have"

Then your internal voice sounds like that. It's not wisdom; it's fear dressed up as practicality.

The brutal truth -- Your parents did their best with the tools they had. But their limitations don't have to become yours.

THE COMPARISON TRAP (AKA SOCIAL MEDIA HELL)

You're comparing your behind-the-scenes to everyone else's highlight reel. Their vacation photos, promotion announcements, and family pictures: all curated, all fiction.

Meanwhile, you're dealing with:

- Credit card debt they don't post about
- Relationship problems they don't share
- Career anxiety they don't admit
- The same 3 AM existential dread everyone has

Reality check: The people who seem to have it all together are also googling "how to adult" at 2 AM.

THE WEIGHT OF BEING "RESPONSIBLE"

You're the one everyone counts on. The reliable one. The one who pays bills on time, shows up when you say you will, and keeps everyone else's shit together.

But who's taking care of your dreams while you're busy being responsible?

Permission slip: You can be responsible AND pursue what you want. They're not mutually exclusive.

THE MAN WHO CRIED IN AISLE 7

The Walmart Breakdown That Changed Everything

Kevin was 44, standing in the cereal aisle at 11 PM, and he couldn't stop crying.

Not the quiet kind of crying you do in your car. The ugly, shoulder-shaking, "someone call security" kind of crying that happens when 20 years of swallowed dreams finally claw their way up your throat.

The setup: Another 14-hour day at the warehouse. Another evening of pretending everything was fine while his wife talked about the kids' college funds they didn't have. Another night of lying in bed calculating how many years until his back gives out completely.

The trigger: His 12-year-old son had asked him at dinner, "Dad, what did you want to be when you grew up?"

His answer: "I wanted to be a chef."

His son's response: "So why aren't you?"

The question that broke him: Because 44-year-old men with mortgages and herniated discs don't get to chase dreams. Because responsible fathers don't risk their families' security on fantasies. Because the window closed when he wasn't looking.

The Walmart moment: He was buying groceries he couldn't afford, thinking about the cooking show he'd watched that morning while getting dressed for a job that was killing him slowly.

The breakdown: Started with one tear. Then five. Then full-body sobs in front of the Cheerios.

The stranger who changed everything: An elderly woman, maybe 70, walked up and said, "Son, whatever it is, it's not too late. I started my restaurant at 67. Still running it at 82."

She handed him a napkin and said: "The only thing worse than starting scared is never starting at all."

Six months later: Kevin isn't running a restaurant. He's working double shifts to save money for culinary school. His back still hurts. The bills are still tight. His wife thinks he's having a midlife crisis.

But here's what changed: Every morning, he gets up 30 minutes early to practice knife cuts. Every Sunday, he cooks one new dish from YouTube. Every night, he falls asleep planning instead of calculating.

Kevin's truth bomb: "I'm not successful yet. I'm not even close. But I'm not dead inside anymore. And that's enough to keep going."

The real lesson: Sometimes the breakdown is the breakthrough. Sometimes crying in public is the most honest thing you've done in years.

HOW TO BUILD SELF-BELIEF WHEN YOU'RE RUNNING ON EMPTY

Start Stupidly Small (Micro-Wins That Actually Work)

Forget "think big." Start microscopic.

- **Monday:** Make your bed before coffee
- **Tuesday:** Speak up once in a meeting
- **Wednesday:** Say no to one thing that drains you
- **Thursday:** Do one thing you've been avoiding for 10 minutes
- **Friday:** Send one message you've been putting off

Why this works: Your mental health needs proof you can trust yourself. Each tiny follow-through builds the foundation.

The Evidence Journal (Your New Best Friend)

Every night, write down:

1. One thing I handled today (even if it was just getting through the day)
2. One moment I didn't give up (even if you wanted to)
3. One thing someone said/did that showed they value me

This isn't toxic positivity. It's data collection. Your brain is wired to notice threats and problems. This rewrites the code.

Breaking Up With Your Inner Critic

That voice in your head telling you you're not enough? It's not the voice of truth; it's the voice of your past trying to keep you safe by keeping you small.

This technique actually works–

- **Name it:** "Anxiety Annie," "Doubt Dave," "Fear Frank"
- **Talk back:** "Thanks for the input, Annie, but I've got this"
- **Redirect:** Replace "I can't" with "I'm learning to"

The "What If I Could?" Game-Changer

When fear says "I can't afford to," ask: "What if I could?"
When doubt says "I'm too old," ask: "What if I'm not?"
When exhaustion says "I don't have time," ask: "What if I made time?"

This isn't about delusional thinking. It's about opening possibilities your fear has shut down.

WHAT TO DO WHEN IT FEELS IMPOSSIBLE

The 2 AM Reality

Some nights, you'll lie awake feeling like you've wasted your life. Like everyone else is ahead. Like you're running out of time.

Truth: Everyone has these nights. Even the people whose lives you envy.

What helps: Remember that feeling behind doesn't mean you're disqualified. It means you're human.

When Everyone Else Seems to Have It Figured Out

Plot twist: They don't.

That colleague who seems so confident? They're googling "how to negotiate salary" just like you.

That friend with the perfect relationship? They're also wondering if they're settling.

That person who "has it all"? They're also questioning their choices at 3 AM.

The relief: You're not broken. You're not behind. You're exactly where millions of other people are — figuring it out as you go.

THE WOMAN WHO STOPPED SAYING "MAYBE I'M CRAZY"

The Conference Call That Broke Her

Rachel was 38, muted on a Zoom call, and having what she would later call her "awakening disguised as a panic attack."

The setup: Third conference call of the day. Another meeting about meetings. Another hour of listening to people who made more money than her explain why her ideas wouldn't work.

The moment: Her boss was presenting Rachel's proposal, word for word, as his own. Again. While she sat there, muted, watching her work get stolen in real time.

Her internal response: "Maybe I'm being dramatic. Maybe I'm remembering wrong. Maybe I'm being too sensitive."

The breaking point: Her boss said, "I think this idea could really revolutionize our approach," and the whole team congratulated him.

The panic attack: Started as chest tightness. Turned into full-body shaking. She hung up, ran to the bathroom, and sat on the floor hyperventilating.

The moment of clarity: Mid-panic attack, she realized she wasn't having a breakdown. She was having a breakthrough. Her body was trying to save her from a life where she made everyone else successful while making herself invisible.

The voice in her head: "You're not crazy. You're just tired of being treated like you're crazy."

What she did next: Called her boss back. Unmuted. And said, "I need to clarify something. That proposal you just presented? I developed that over the past six weeks. I have the emails and drafts to prove it."

The silence: 8 seconds of pure terror.

His response: "Rachel, I think you're confused. We developed this together in our meeting last week."

Her response: "No, Jim. I'm not confused. I'm done."

The aftermath: She didn't quit that day. She couldn't afford to. But she started documenting everything. Every idea. Every meeting. Every time she was interrupted, overlooked, or erased.

Three months later: Armed with evidence, she filed a formal complaint. Not because she was brave. Because she was desperate.

The result: Jim was "restructured" out of his position. Rachel got his job. The promotion she'd been told wasn't possible suddenly became possible.

Rachel's truth bomb: "I spent three years thinking I was paranoid. Turns out I was just observant. The gaslighting was so consistent I started gaslighting myself."

> **The real lesson:** Sometimes what feels like a panic attack is actually your truth trying to claw its way out.

Building Your "I See You" Circle

You need at least one person who believes in you when you forget how. Not someone who gives empty encouragement, but someone who sees your potential and won't let you shrink.

Warning: Limit time with people who:

- Always have a reason why your ideas won't work

- Make you feel guilty for wanting more

- Need you to stay small so they feel better about themselves.

THE REAL TALK

You Don't Need Permission, But Here It Is Anyway

Permission to:

- Want more than what you have

- Change your mind about the path you're on

- Disappoint people who've gotten comfortable with your limitations

- Take up space

- Ask for what you need

- Be tired of being "grateful" for situations that drain you.

The Uncomfortable Truth About Starting Over

Starting over at 28 is different from starting over at 38. The stakes feel higher. The safety net feels thinner. The criticism feels louder.

But here's what's also true: You have experience now. Perspective. Skills. Screw-up tolerance. That 22-year-old version of you was naive. This version of you is seasoned. Use it.

What Self-Belief Actually Looks Like

It's not waking up feeling confident every day. It's:

- Applying for jobs you're not 100% qualified for
- Having the hard conversation even when your voice shakes
- Choosing the unknown over the comfortable-but-soul-sucking
- Betting on yourself even when the odds look shitty.

YOUR NEW OPERATING SYSTEM

Old belief: "I need to feel ready before I can move forward"
New reality: "Readiness is a luxury I can't afford to wait for"

Old belief: "I should be further along by now"
New reality: "I'm exactly where I need to be to get where I'm going"

Old belief: "Everyone else has advantages I don't have"
New reality: "Everyone else is also making it up as they go along"

Old belief: "I've already tried and failed"
New reality: "I've already survived failure, which means I can handle whatever comes next"

THE BOTTOM LINE

Self-belief isn't about thinking you're amazing. It's about trusting that you can handle whatever happens next.

You've already survived every bad day you've had so far. Every disappointment. Every failure. Every moment you thought would break you.

That's not luck. That's evidence.

You don't need to feel ready. You don't need to have it all figured out. You don't need anyone's permission.

You just need to trust that you can figure it out as you go.

Because here's the thing they don't tell you: Everyone else is doing that exact same thing.

The only difference between people who change their lives and people who don't isn't confidence, connections, or even luck.

It's the willingness to start before they feel ready.

Your move.

THE CHALLENGE:

THE 30-DAY STOP-ABANDONING-YOURSELF EXPERIMENT

Warning: This Will Feel Like Dying (But It's Actually Living)

This isn't about building confidence. This is about stopping the slow-motion suicide of abandoning yourself to keep everyone else comfortable.

Step 1: THE RECOGNITION

Your mission: Start documenting your self-abandonment.

Daily practice:

- **Morning:** Write down one way you'll probably abandon yourself today
- **Evening:** Write down whether you did it and how it felt

The brutal questions:

- "When did I make myself smaller today?"
- "What did I pretend not to need?"
- "What did I not say that needed saying?"

The point: You can't stop a pattern you won't acknowledge.

Step 2: THE INTERRUPTION

Your mission: Catch yourself mid-abandonment and course-correct.

Daily practice:

- **Catch yourself** saying "It's fine" when it's not fine
- **Stop mid-sentence** and tell the truth: "Actually, it's not fine"
- **One truth bomb:** Every day, say one thing you've been avoiding

The uncomfortable reality: People are used to you abandoning yourself. They won't like it when you stop.

The point: Their discomfort with your authenticity is not your problem.

Step 3: THE REBELLION

Your mission: Stop asking permission to have needs.

Daily practice:

- **One boundary:** Set one boundary without over-explaining it
- **One need:** Ask for one thing without justifying why you deserve it

- **One truth:** Share one feeling without apologizing for having it

The pushback: People will call you selfish, difficult, or "changed." That's how you know it's working.

The point: You're not becoming someone different. You're becoming someone who doesn't abandon themselves.

Step 4: THE INTEGRATION

Your mission: Make self-loyalty your default setting.

Daily practice:

- **Morning question:** "How can I be loyal to myself today?"
- **Midday check-in:** "Am I abandoning myself right now?"
- **Evening audit:** "What evidence did I create today that I'm on my own side?"

The shift: Stop asking "What will people think?" Start asking "What will I think of myself?"

THE BREAKDOWN MOMENT

It will happen pretty soon. You'll feel like you're being selfish. Like you're hurting people. Like you're becoming someone nobody will love.

That's the moment your old programming is fighting back. It's not true. It's just loud.

The truth: You're not becoming selfish. You're becoming self-loyal. There's a difference.

THE BREAKTHROUGH MOMENT

Shortly after, you'll realize you've stopped apologizing for existing. You'll catch yourself automatically assuming you have a right to take up space.

That's the moment you realize self-belief was never about becoming more confident. It was about stopping the voice that convinced you that you were less important than everyone else.

THE REAL CHALLENGE

Don't warn people. Don't explain what you're doing. Don't prepare them for your changes.

Why this matters: Your old self would have asked permission to stop abandoning yourself. Your new self just stops.

WHAT YOU'LL DISCOVER

- You've been making yourself smaller for decades
- Most people's "needs" are actually preferences
- You're more resilient than your people-pleasing suggests
- The voice that says "you're being selfish" gets quieter when you stop feeding it

THE TRUTH THEY DON'T TELL YOU

This won't make you popular. It will make you real.

You won't become more confident. You'll become more honest about the confidence you already have.

You won't stop caring what people think. You'll stop letting their opinions override your needs.

THE UNCOMFORTABLE REALITY

In a matter of weeks from now, some relationships will be different. Some people will be uncomfortable with your authenticity.

But here's what else will happen: You'll sleep better. You'll breathe easier. You'll look in the mirror and recognize yourself.

The real revolution: You'll realize you were never broken. You were just well-trained in self-abandonment.

Stop making yourself smaller to make others comfortable.

Your move.

CHAPTER EIGHT

THE RAGE YOU CAN'T EXPRESS IS EATING YOU ALIVE.

STOP EMOTIONAL STARVATION BEFORE IT KILLS EVERYTHING YOU CARE ABOUT.

You're holding it together. Smile at the boss who treats you like shit. Nod when your partner lists everything you're doing wrong. Stay calm when the bills pile up and the future looks bleak. Keep your mouth shut when your kids push every button you have.

But inside? You're screaming.

And that scream, the one you swallow every day, is destroying you from the inside out.

It's not just stress. It's not just being tired. It's emotional starvation.

You've been managing everyone else's feelings for so long, your own are dying of neglect.

Here's what nobody tells you about emotions:

When you starve them, they don't disappear. They go underground. They turn toxic. And they wait.

Until one day, you explode at your 8-year-old for spilling juice. Or you tell your spouse exactly what you think, at 2 AM, in the worst possible way. Or you walk into your boss's office and burn everything down.

Then you hate yourself for it. Call it stress. Promise to do better. And go back to swallowing the scream.

That's not strength.

ELENA'S PERFECT FUNERAL

Elena buried her daughter on a Tuesday and went back to work on Wednesday.

Not because she was strong. Because she was terrified of what would happen if she stopped moving.

Sophia died at 16 in a car accident that wasn't anyone's fault—a patch of black ice, a moment of physics that changed everything. Elena's only child, gone in an instant that felt both impossible and inevitable.

The funeral was perfect. Elena planned every detail while relatives whispered about how "well she was handling it." She chose flowers, wrote the program, delivered a eulogy that made everyone cry while she stayed dry-eyed and composed.

"She's being so brave," people said.

Elena wasn't brave. She was holding her breath underwater, and everyone was congratulating her on her swimming technique.

For six months after Sophia's death, Elena functioned flawlessly. She returned to her job as an ER nurse. The same job where she'd learned to compartmentalize trauma, to function through crisis, to save other people's children while her own lay in the ground.

She answered sympathy cards with handwritten thank-you notes. Attended grief counselling sessions where she listened to other parents fall apart while offering them tissues. Made Sophia's favourite pasta every Sunday and ate it alone, mechanically, like medicine.

Everyone praised her strength. Her resilience. Her grace under unimaginable pressure.

The breaking point came during a routine shift in the ER. A 16-year-old girl came in after a car accident—minor injuries, mostly scared. Her mother was hysterical, sobbing and clutching the girl's hand while Elena checked her vitals.

"I can't lose her," the mother kept saying. "I can't lose her."

Something crystallized in Elena's chest. Something sharp and deadly that had been building for six months.

"You won't," Elena said, her voice steady and professional. "She's going to be fine."

But the mother couldn't stop crying, couldn't stop saying it: "I can't lose her. I can't lose her."

Elena set down her stethoscope and looked directly at the woman.

"You can," she said quietly. "You absolutely can lose her. It can happen in a second, on a random Tuesday, for no reason at all. And when it does, everyone will tell you how strong you are while you die inside. They'll praise you for functioning while you forget how to breathe. So stop wasting time being scared and start being grateful she's here right now."

The room went silent. The mother stared at Elena with shock and hurt. The teenage girl looked terrified.

Elena walked out of the room, out of the ER, and didn't stop walking until she reached her car. Then she sat in the parking lot and screamed until her throat was raw.

Six months of perfect composure shattered in a single, brutal moment of truth.

She was fired the next day. Not for being wrong, but for being human at the wrong time.

Three years later, Elena works at a hospice. She helps families say goodbye to their loved ones, and she tells them the truth: grief isn't supposed to be graceful. It's supposed to be devastating.

Her colleagues think she's excellent at her job because she's "been through it." They don't know that every day, she's learning how to breathe again. That she still makes Sophia's pasta on Sundays, but now she cries while she eats it.

> The explosion in that ER wasn't a breakdown. It was a resurrection.
>
> Elena had been so busy being everyone else's idea of a grieving mother that she'd forgotten to actually grieve.

THE LIE THAT'S KEEPING YOU TRAPPED

"Real men don't let emotions control them." Or "That's not lady-Like"

So you buried them. Ignored them. Told yourself they were weakness.

But here's the brutal truth:

Your emotions aren't controlling you – your fear of them is.

Every time you stuff down frustration, it becomes resentment. Every time you ignore exhaustion, it becomes rage. Every time you deny fear, it becomes paralysis.

You think you're being strong. You're actually bleeding out.

And the people around you? They feel it.

Your partner feels the wall you've built. Your kids feel the tension you think you're hiding. Your coworkers see the fake smile that doesn't reach your eyes.

You're not protecting anyone. You're poisoning everything.

WHY 'JUST THINK POSITIVE' IS BULLSHIT

How many times have you been told:

"Don't let it get to you." "Stay positive." "Everything happens for a reason."

While you're drowning in a dead-end job. While your marriage feels like roommates with benefits. While you're one emergency away from financial disaster.

That advice isn't just useless; it's insulting.

Your reality genuinely sucks in some ways. And that's okay.

You don't need to think positive. You need to think clearly. About what you're actually feeling. About why you're feeling it. About what to do with it before it destroys everything.

WHAT EMOTIONAL SURVIVAL ACTUALLY LOOKS LIKE

Forget "emotional intelligence." This is about **emotional triage.**

When you're overwhelmed, broke, and running on empty, you need to:

1. **Stop the bleeding** - Identify what's actually killing you inside
2. **Stabilize the patient** - Learn to feel without exploding
3. **Assess the damage** - Figure out what needs immediate attention
4. **Survive today** - Get through without making things worse
5. **Plan the recovery** - Start rebuilding from the inside out

This isn't therapy. This isn't self-help jargon. This is combat medicine for your emotional life.

THE CHALLENGE

THE FOUR EMOTIONS THAT ARE DESTROYING YOUR LIFE

1. The Rage You're Not Allowed to Have

You're angry. At your job that treats you like a number. At bills that never stop coming. At a world that promised you more and delivered less. At yourself for not being further along by now.

And you're not allowed to say it.

So it turns into:

- Sarcasm that cuts deeper than you mean
- Passive-aggression that confuses everyone
- Depression that feels like concrete in your chest
- Explosions at the people who matter most

The truth: Your anger isn't the problem. Your shame about it is.

Tool: Anger Audit Once a week, write down:

- What am I actually pissed about?
- What's underneath the anger? (Usually fear or hurt)
- What would I say if I could say anything?
- What needs to change, and what's just life being life?

Don't edit. Don't judge. Just bleed on paper.

2. The Fear You Can't Admit

You're scared.

That this is as good as it gets. That you'll never have enough money. That your kids will struggle like you do. That you're wasting your life in a job that doesn't matter. That you're failing at being a person, a partner, a parent.

But fear isn't acceptable.

So you call it:

- "Being realistic"
- "Planning ahead"
- "Staying focused"

While inside, you're terrified.

Tool: Fear Translation When you catch yourself "being realistic," ask:

- What am I actually afraid of?
- Is this fear protecting me or paralyzing me?
- What would I do if I wasn't scared?
- What's the smallest step I could take toward that?

3. The Exhaustion That Nobody Sees

You're tired. Not sleepy tired. Soul tired.

Tired of pretending everything's fine. Tired of being the strong one. Tired of having the answers. Tired of carrying everyone else's emotional weight.

But exhaustion looks like laziness to everyone else.

So you push through. Drink more coffee. Sleep less. Ignore the warning signs.

Until your body forces you to stop.

Tool: The Energy Audit Every day for a week, track:

- What drained me today?
- What gave me energy?
- Who did I manage emotionally?
- When did I actually rest vs just collapse?

You'll be shocked at how much emotional labor you're doing.

4. The Shame That Never Stops Talking

You're not where you thought you'd be by now. You're not the person you imagined becoming. You're not providing like you promised. You're not as patient, successful, or together as you should be.

And that voice in your head won't shut up.

"Other people figure this out." "You're behind." "You should be better at this."

That shame is killing your confidence, your relationships, and your ability to make good decisions.

Tool: Shame vs. Reality Check When the shame spiral starts:

- What story am I telling myself?
- What would I tell my best friend in this situation?
- What's actually true vs what's just my inner critic?
- What's one thing I've handled well recently?

THE REAL REASON YOU EXPLODE AT YOUR FAMILY

It's not because they're difficult. It's not because you're a bad person.

It's because they're safe.

Your boss can fire you, so you bite your tongue. Your friends might judge you, so you stay positive. Society expects you to be strong, so you fake it.

But your family? They have to love you anyway. So they get the anger meant for your boss. The fear you can't show at work. The exhaustion you hide from everyone else.

They're not the problem. They're the pressure valve.

And that's destroying the relationships that matter most.

The Year She Stopped Being Nice

Anna's feet had been screaming for three days.

It was 4:47 PM on Thanksgiving Day, and sixteen people were crammed into her house- her house that she'd cleaned, her table she'd set, her food she'd been preparing since Monday. Her hands were raw and bleeding from washing dishes. She'd eaten nothing but stolen bites while cooking for others, her stomach a knot of acid and resentment.

She'd been up since 4 AM, fueled by caffeine and the bone-deep exhaustion of someone who'd been emotionally feeding sixteen people while starving herself.

"Anna dear," her mother-in-law Linda said, cutting into the turkey with surgical precision, "I think this is a little dry. You know, I offered to help, but you always insist on doing everything yourself. I just worry you're taking on too much."

The fake concern. The rewriting of history. The way Linda made Anna's martyrdom sound like Anna's choice.

Anna had been choking down Linda's backhanded criticism for seventeen years. Seventeen years of Christmas dinners where Linda pointed out the spots on the silverware. Seventeen years of Easter brunches where Linda suggested Anna might want to "try a different approach" to the ham.

Seventeen years of being the family's emotional servant while everyone else disappeared into football games and wine.

"Actually, Linda," Anna said, setting down her carving knife, "the turkey is perfectly fine."

The conversations around the table stuttered to a halt. Mark, her husband, looked up from his phone with the expression of someone who'd just heard a bomb tick.

"I'm sorry?" Linda's voice carried the particular chill of a woman who'd never been contradicted.

"I said the turkey is fine. And I didn't insist on doing everything myself. I've been begging for help for seventeen years. You've just been too busy criticizing to actually contribute."

Anna could feel her children staring. Her thirteen-year-old daughter, Sophie, had grown up watching this dance—women serving, men disappearing, everyone taking Anna's labor for granted. This was what Sophie thought love looked like.

"Anna," Mark's voice cut through the silence like a blade, "what the hell is wrong with you? You're embarrassing yourself. This is my family—MY family—and you're acting like a psychopath."

Something crystallized in Anna's chest. Something sharp and deadly that had been building for seventeen years.

"Your family," she repeated slowly. "Your family that I've been hosting for seventeen years. Your family that I've been cooking for, cleaning for, managing the emotions of. Your family that shows up empty-handed every year and leaves me with a kitchen that looks like a war zone."

She stood up, her chair scraping against the floor.

"Linda, you've been criticizing my cooking for seventeen years while contributing nothing but complaints. You've never brought a dish, never helped clean, never said thank you. You show up, eat food I killed myself to make, and then tell me how I could have done it better. You're not helpful—you're parasitic."

The turkey sat between them like evidence at a crime scene.

"And Mark," Anna turned to her husband, her voice steady despite the earthquake in her chest, "you disappear every holiday. You invite your family to my house, leave me to manage all of it alone, and then tell me I'm embarrassing when I finally crack. You don't want a wife—you want a caterer who sleeps with you."

Seventeen years of swallowed words poured out of her like blood from a wound.

"I'm done," she said, looking around the table at faces that had watched her slowly disappear. "I'm done pretending this is normal. I'm done being grateful for the privilege of serving people who don't even like me. I'm done being nice."

She walked upstairs to her bedroom and locked the door.

Three family members never spoke to her again. Linda told everyone Anna had "lost her mind" and needed "professional help." Mark's sister

109

started hosting holidays at her house and didn't invite Anna. The kids had to choose sides at every birthday party.

Some relationships died that day—not because Anna was wrong, but because she'd stopped being convenient.

But Sophie, her thirteen-year-old daughter, knocked on the bedroom door an hour later.

"Mom?" she whispered. "Are you okay?"

Anna opened the door to find Sophie holding two plates of food.

"I saved you some turkey," Sophie said. "And I think you were right. It's not dry at all."

Two years later, Anna still has panic attacks before family gatherings. Not because she regrets the explosion, but because she realizes how close she came to disappearing completely. She'd been practicing emotional suicide for so long that the explosion was the only thing that saved her life.

The real horror wasn't what she said. It was what she'd been swallowing for years.

THE SANITY CHECK (BEFORE YOU LOSE YOUR SHIT)

When you feel yourself about to explode, ask these five questions:

1. **What am I actually feeling right now?** (Not "stressed"; be specific)

2. **Who or what is this feeling really about?** (Usually not the person in front of you)

3. **What do I need right now?** (Space, respect, help, acknowledgment)

4. **What will happen if I react from this feeling?** (Honest assessment)

5. **What do I want the outcome to be?** (Connection or just venting?)

This takes 30 seconds. It can save your marriage.

WHY YOUR EMOTIONS ARE TRYING TO SAVE YOU

You've been taught that emotions are the enemy. That they make you weak. That successful people don't have them.

That's backwards.

Your emotions are data. They're your internal GPS. They're trying to tell you something important.

- **Anger** says: "Something needs to change"
- **Fear** says: "Pay attention to this"
- **Sadness** says: "This matters to me"
- **Exhaustion** says: "You need to stop"

When you ignore them, you're flying blind. Making decisions without crucial information. No wonder you keep ending up in the same struggles.

THE EMOTIONAL TRIAGE SYSTEM

When you're overwhelmed, you need priorities. You can't fix everything at once. You need triage.

Level 1: Stop the Bleeding

- What emotion is about to make me do something stupid?
- What's the minimum I need to do to get through today?
- Who needs me to be stable right now?

Level 2: Stabilize

- What's driving the crisis feeling?
- What support do I actually need?
- What can wait until I'm thinking clearly?

Level 3: Rebuild

- What patterns keep putting me here?
- What boundaries do I need to set?
- What needs to change long-term?

THE THREE-MINUTE EMOTIONAL RESET

When you're about to lose it:

Minute 1: Name it "I'm furious that..." "I'm scared about..." "I'm exhausted from..."

Minute 2: Breathe it Six deep breaths. Feel where the emotion sits in your body. Don't try to fix it, just notice it.

Minute 3: Choose it What do I want to happen next? What version of myself do I want to be? What's one thing I can do that aligns with that?

This isn't magic. It's giving your thinking brain time to come back online.

WHY THIS ISN'T SOFT. IT'S SURVIVAL.

Think about it:

The persons who stay married? They learned to fight without destroying.

The ones who advance at work? They stay calm under pressure.

Those who earned their kids respect? They don't explode every time life gets hard.

This isn't about being sensitive. It's about being effective.

When you can feel without falling apart:

- You make better decisions under pressure
- People trust you with the hard stuff

- Your relationships get stronger, not weaker
- Your kids learn emotional strength from watching you
- You stop sabotaging everything you build

THE EMOTION THAT'S HARDER THAN ANGER

It's not rage that destroys people. It's numbness.

When you've stuffed feelings down for so long, you stop feeling anything. Your marriage becomes routine. Your kids become obligations. Your dreams become fantasies.

You're alive, but you're not living.

And that's when you really lose everything.

```
┌─────────────────────────────────────────────┐
│                 THE CHALLENGE                 │
└─────────────────────────────────────────────┘
```

HOW TO START FEELING AGAIN (WITHOUT FALLING APART)

Start small.

Pick one emotion per week. Just notice when it shows up. Don't fix it, change it, or judge it. Just: "There's anger" or "There's fear."

Step 1: *Notice anger (frustration, irritation, resentment)*

Step 2: *Notice fear (worry, anxiety, dread)*

Step 3: *Notice sadness (disappointment, grief, loneliness)*

Step 4: *Notice joy (satisfaction, hope, connection)*

By month's end, you'll have emotional vocabulary again. And vocabulary is the first step to power.

THE ONE THING THAT CHANGES EVERYTHING

Stop apologizing for having emotions.

To yourself. To others. To the world.

You're not broken for feeling overwhelmed. You're not weak for being scared. You're not bad for getting angry.

You're human.

And humans who acknowledge their humanity? They're the ones who actually change their lives.

THE HIDDEN STRENGTH

Every person who's built something lasting learned this:

Your emotions aren't what make you weak. Your relationship with them is.

When you can feel fear and act anyway, that's courage. When you can feel anger and respond wisely, that's power. When you can feel sadness and still show up, that's strength.

The goal isn't to feel less. It's to fear your feelings less.

FINAL TOOL: THE DAILY EMOTIONAL CHECK-IN

Before bed, ask yourself:

1. What did I feel most strongly today?
2. What was that feeling trying to tell me?
3. How did I handle it?
4. What do I want to do differently tomorrow?

Write it down. One or two sentences. No judgment.

After 30 days, you'll see patterns. After 90 days, you'll have choices. After a year, you'll have a different life.

Not because you stopped feeling. Because you stopped being afraid of what you feel.

THE PROMISE

You'll stop surviving your emotions and start using them.

That's not self-help. That's self-rescue.

And it's the difference between a life you endure and a life you actually live.

THE DEVASTATING TRUTH

Both Sarah and Anna were choosing between survival and soul-death.

They weren't having bad days. They weren't being difficult.

They were practicing emotional suicide—slowly, quietly, professionally, politely—until their souls staged an intervention.

The explosions weren't breakdowns. They were resurrections.

The real tragedy isn't that they lost some relationships. It's that they almost lost themselves.

And the people who punished them for refusing to be convenient? They were never really supporting them anyway.

The choice isn't between being nice and being difficult. It's between being authentic and being dead inside.

That's the devastating truth about emotional starvation. The alternative to explosion isn't peace.

It's disappearing completely.

CHAPTER NINE

THE POWER OF MINDSET

REWIRING HOW YOU THINK, FEEL AND WIN

Your Mind Is Either Your Prison or Your Key.

Do you know that voice in your head?

The one that says you're falling behind while everyone else has it figured out? The one that turns a simple work email into evidence that you're about to get fired? The one that makes you scroll your phone for two hours because even choosing what to watch on Netflix feels like too much work?

That voice isn't you. It's programming. And most of it was installed without your permission.

Here's what nobody tells you about mindset work: It's not about thinking positive thoughts while your life is on fire. It's about changing how you respond when everything feels impossible (which, let's be honest, is most days).

THE REAL PROBLEM NOBODY TALKS ABOUT

You've probably tried the mindset thing before. Maybe you bought a journal that's now collecting dust. Maybe you downloaded a meditation app that still sends you guilt-inducing notifications. Maybe you even went to therapy and got told to "reframe your thoughts" while drowning in student loans and dealing with a boss who texts you at 11 PM.

Here's why none of that worked: Most mindset advice assumes you have mental energy left over. It assumes you're not already running on fumes, trying to hold together a job you hate, relationships that drain you, and a bank account that gives you anxiety every time you check it.

This isn't about adding more to your plate. This is about changing the plate entirely.

YOU'RE NOT BROKEN. YOU'RE JUST RUNNING BAD SOFTWARE

Ever feel like you can't get your shit together? That's not character weakness. That's an internal system that was programmed for a different world.

You were built to survive immediate physical threats, not navigate performance reviews, social media comparisons, and the anxiety of wondering if you'll ever afford a house. Your brain treats your mortgage payment like a saber-toothed tiger, which is why you lie awake at 3 AM with your heart racing about things you can't control.

Here's what's actually happening in your head:

Your phone buzzes with a work email at 9 PM. Your system doesn't think "email." It thinks "DANGER." Your body floods with the same chemicals it would release if you were being chased by a predator. Except there's nowhere to run, so you just... sit there, wired and exhausted at the same time.

You spill coffee on your clothes before an important meeting. Instead of thinking "minor inconvenience," your brain goes straight to "This is proof I'm a disaster and everyone's going to notice and I'm going to get fired and lose my apartment."

Sound familiar? That's not you being dramatic. That's programming. And like any software, it can be updated.

THE TWO TYPES OF PEOPLE (AND WHICH ONE YOU ARE)

Type 1: The Reactor

- Life happens TO them
- Every problem feels personal
- Constantly waiting for things to get easier
- Thinks "I'll be happy when..." (I get promoted, lose weight, meet someone, pay off debt)
- Believes their thoughts are facts

Type 2: The Responder

- Life happens, they choose their response
- Problems are puzzles, not punishments
- Expects life to be hard and plans accordingly
- Thinks "I'll be happy while..." (figuring this out, building something, becoming stronger)
- Knows their thoughts are just thoughts

You were probably raised to be Type 1. Most of us were. But Type 2 is learnable, if you're willing to get uncomfortable.

STORY ONE: THE WOMAN WHO DISCOVERED SHE DIDN'T EXIST

The Mirror That Shattered Everything

Lisa was 34, standing in her bathroom at 2:47 AM on a Tuesday, staring at her reflection after another sleepless night, when she realized she had never actually met herself.

The setup: Another night of lying awake, mind racing with the same recursive loop that had been running for years. The promotion she didn't get. The relationship that ended. The weight she couldn't lose. The life that felt like it was happening to someone else while she watched from the sidelines.

The trigger: She'd gotten up to pee and caught sight of herself in the mirror. Not a glance - a full stop, face-to-face encounter with a stranger who looked exactly like her.

The moment everything broke: She heard herself think, Who the fuck is that person?

The spiral: That's me. That's supposedly me. But I don't recognize her. I don't recognize anything about her. She looks tired. She looks defeated. She looks like someone who's been pretending to be someone else for so long she forgot who she was pretending to be.

The awakening: Wait. If I don't recognize myself, then who has been living my life? Who has been making my decisions? Who has been thinking my thoughts?

The realization that shattered everything: I've been living as a collection of other people's expectations. My mother's voice telling me to be responsible. My ex's voice telling me I'm not enough. My boss's voice telling me to be grateful. Society's voice telling me what success looks like. I've been a fucking echo chamber.

The terror: If I'm not any of those voices, then who am I? If I strip away everything I've been told I should be, what's left? What if there's nothing left?

The physical reality: Her reflection started to feel foreign. Like she was looking at a stranger wearing her face. Her hands were shaking. Her breathing was shallow. The bathroom felt like it was tilting.

119

The breakdown: She started laughing. Not happy laughter - the kind of laughter that happens when your mind breaks and you realize the joke has been on you your entire life.

The moment of truth: I've been so busy being the person I thought I should be that I never asked who I actually am. I've been so busy managing everyone else's opinion of me that I never formed my own opinion of me. I've been so busy living up to standards that I never questioned if they were my standards.

What she did next: She sat on the bathroom floor at 3 AM and asked herself a question she'd never asked before: If nobody else's opinion mattered - not my parents, not my ex, not society, not anyone - what would I want my life to look like?

The silence: The answer didn't come immediately. Because she'd never asked the question before. She'd been so busy being a good daughter, a good employee, a good girlfriend, a good citizen, that she'd never been anything for herself.

The shift: I've been living someone else's life in my body. I've been an actor playing a role I never auditioned for. But the script was never mine. The character was never mine. Even the dreams were never mine.

The aftermath: She didn't quit her job the next day. She didn't dramatically change her life. But she started asking different questions. Not "What should I do?" but "What do I want to do?" Not "What will people think?" but "What do I think?"

Six months later: Lisa was still figuring out who she was. But she'd stopped being who she wasn't. She'd stopped living for the approval of people whose opinions she'd never actually respected.

The real change: When people asked her what she wanted, she stopped automatically saying "I don't know" and started saying "I'm still figuring that out." The difference was everything.

Lisa's truth bomb: "I spent 34 years being a perfectly programmed robot. Following instructions I never agreed to. Living a life I never chose. The scariest part wasn't realizing I didn't know who I was. The scariest part was realizing I'd never even asked."

The real lesson: Most people are living someone else's life in their own body. They're following a script they never wrote, playing a character they

> never chose, pursuing goals they never wanted. The person you think you are might not be you at all.

The "Holy Shit, That's Me" Test

Before we go any further, let's check if this is really your problem:

☐ You know exactly what you should do (exercise, meal prep, call your mom, update your resume) but can't make yourself do it.

☐ You're more productive during your lunch break than the entire morning because those 30 minutes are actually yours.

☐ You fantasize about winning the lottery not for the mansion, but for the permission to finally rest.

☐ You have imaginary arguments with your boss, your ex, or that person who cut you off in traffic.

☐ You check your phone the moment you wake up, even though you hate starting your day that way.

☐ You feel guilty about being tired when you "haven't really done anything."

☐ You compare your behind-the-scenes to everyone else's highlight reel and wonder why you can't get it together.

If you checked more than three boxes, keep reading. This is fixable.

The Real Mindset Shift (Not the Bullshit Version)

Forget what you've heard about "positive thinking." This isn't about pretending your problems don't exist. This is about changing how you interpret what happens to you.

Same situation, different programming

Your boss gives you negative feedback

Old programming: "I'm terrible at this job. I'm going to get fired. I knew I wasn't smart enough for this position. My parents were right about me."

New programming: "This feedback sucks to hear, but it's information. I can either use it to get better or find a job where I'm a better fit. Either way, I'm not going to let someone else's opinion become my identity."

The difference isn't optimism vs. pessimism. It's ownership vs. victimhood.

Tool #1: The Bullshit Detector Method

Your thoughts lie to you constantly. Most of them aren't even yours; they're just recycled worry, inherited anxiety, and social media programming running on repeat.

When you catch yourself spiraling:

1. **Stop and name it:** "I'm having the 'I'm a failure' thought again" or "I'm having the 'nothing ever works out for me' thought."

2. **Ask the magic question:** "Is this thought helping me solve the problem or just making me feel worse?"

3. **Choose a response:** "This thought isn't useful right now. What would be useful?"

Let's review some examples:

- **Old thought**: "I'm so far behind everyone else"
- **Bullshit detector:** This is the comparison trap again
- **New response:** "I'm exactly where I need to be to learn what I need to learn"

- **Old thought:** "I'll never figure this out"
- **Bullshit detector:** This is fortune-telling based on fear
- **New response:** "I haven't figured this out YET"

Tool #2: The Emergency Reset (For When Everything Feels Impossible)

Some days, you don't need a morning routine. You need life support. This is for those days when getting out of bed feels like climbing Mount Everest.

When you're overwhelmed to the point of paralysis:

1. **Breathe like your life depends on it** (4 counts in, 6 counts out, repeat 5 times)
2. **Name one thing that's actually okay right now** ("I have food in my fridge," "My dog is healthy," "I made it through yesterday")
3. **Pick the smallest possible win** (brush teeth, drink water, send one email)
4. **Do that thing**
5. **Give yourself credit for doing it.**

This isn't about productivity. This is about proving to that inner person that you're still capable of forward motion, even when everything feels stuck.

STORY TWO: THE MAN WHO WAS ADDICTED TO HIS OWN SUFFERING

The Moment He Understood His Pain Was His Drug

Jordan was 38, sitting in his therapist's office at 4:00 PM on a Thursday, describing his problems for the 47th time in 18 months, when he realized he was in love with his own misery.

The setup: Another session. Another hour of explaining why his life wasn't working. Another $150 spent cataloging his trauma, his anxiety, his depression, his inability to maintain relationships, his career struggles, his financial stress.

The routine: He'd been telling the same stories for a year and a half. The absent father. The critical mother. The ex-wife who left him. The job that didn't appreciate him. The friends who didn't understand him. The world that was against him.

The trigger: His therapist, Dr. Chen, interrupted him mid-sentence. "Jordan, what would happen if your problems were solved?"

The question that broke everything: What would happen if my problems were solved?

The spiral: If my problems were solved... I wouldn't have anything to talk about. I wouldn't have a reason to come here. I wouldn't have anything to explain to people. I wouldn't have anything to blame for why my life isn't working. I wouldn't have... I wouldn't have an identity.

The realization: Holy shit. I'm terrified of not having problems. I'm terrified of being okay. Because if I'm okay, then I have to be responsible for what happens next. If I'm okay, then I can't blame my past for my present. If I'm okay, then I have to actually live instead of just surviving.

The moment everything shattered: I've been treating my problems like they're happening TO me. But what if... what if I'm happening to them? What if I'm keeping them alive because they're the only thing that makes me feel special? What if my suffering is the only thing that makes me interesting?

The physical reality: His chest felt hollow. His hands started trembling. The room felt like it was spinning. He could hear his own heartbeat.

The breakdown: I'm addicted to my own pain. I'm addicted to being the victim. I'm addicted to being broken because being broken means I don't have to be accountable for being whole.

The terror: If I'm not the guy with problems, then who am I? If I'm not the victim of my circumstances, then I'm the author of them. If I'm not broken, then I'm responsible for fixing what's not working. If I'm not suffering, then I have to start succeeding.

The moment of truth: I've been using my past as a drug. Every time I feel scared about the future, I shoot up with stories about how I was wronged. Every time I feel pressure to change, I get high on reasons why I can't. Every time someone expects something from me, I overdose on excuses.

What he did next: He looked at Dr. Chen and said, "I think I'm addicted to being fucked up."

The response: "What would happen if you went into recovery?"

The shift: Recovery would mean... letting go of the stories that keep me small. Recovery would mean... stop using my past as a reason to not have a future. Recovery would mean... being okay with being okay.

The aftermath: He didn't magically become healed. But he started catching himself. When he began telling the familiar stories, he'd stop and ask: "Am I sharing this to heal or to stay stuck?"

The real change: He started treating his problems like visitors, not permanent residents. When anxiety showed up, instead of setting up a room for it, he'd say, "Thanks for stopping by. You don't live here anymore."

Six months later: Jordan still had problems. But he'd stopped being professionally broken. He'd stopped introducing himself through his trauma. He'd stopped making his pain his personality.

The relationship shift: He stopped choosing friends who wanted to hear his problems and started choosing friends who wanted to hear his progress.

Jordan's truth bomb: "I realized I was a trauma junkie. I was addicted to my own suffering because it gave me something to talk about, something to blame, something to hide behind. The scariest thing wasn't healing. The scariest thing was realizing I didn't want to heal because being broken was easier than being responsible."

The real lesson: Some people are addicted to their own problems. They're so identified with their pain that healing feels like dying. They're so comfortable with dysfunction that function feels dangerous. They're so used to being victims that being powerful feels like betrayal.

The uncomfortable truth: Your problems might be your identity. Your suffering might be your safety blanket. Your brokenness might be your brand. And letting go of them might be the most terrifying thing you ever do.

THE IDENTITY PROBLEM (WHY WILLPOWER ALWAYS FAILS)

Here's the thing nobody tells you: You will always act like the person you believe you are.

If you believe you're "someone who can't stick to anything," you'll find a way to prove that true. If you believe you're "not a morning person," you'll hit snooze. If you believe you're "bad with money," you'll make financial decisions that confirm it.

This isn't conscious self-sabotage. This is your identity protecting itself.

The question isn't "What do I want to do?" The question is "Who do I want to be?"

Tool #3: Identity Shift Protocol

Instead of trying to change behaviors, change your identity. The behaviors will follow.

Step 1: Define your next-level identity in one sentence

Not "I want to be successful" (too vague). Try: "I'm someone who honors commitments to myself" or "I'm someone who solves problems instead of avoiding them."

Step 2: Collect evidence

Every time you do something that proves this identity true, write it down. Even tiny things count.

- "I said I'd drink more water and I did"
- "I felt anxious about that phone call but made it anyway"

- "I wanted to scroll but did the dishes instead"

Step 3: Act from the identity, not toward it

Instead of "I'm trying to become disciplined," try "I'm disciplined, so what would I do right now?"

THE 12-MINUTE MORNING (FOR PEOPLE WHO DON'T HAVE TIME)

Forget elaborate morning routines. You need something that works when you have 12 minutes before the kids wake up or you have to catch the train.

Minutes 1-3: Get present No phone. Just breathe. Notice you're alive and conscious. That's actually pretty wild when you think about it.

Minutes 4-6: Remember who you are Say your identity statement out loud. "I'm someone who..." Feel free to whisper if people are sleeping.

Minutes 7-9: Plan your win What's ONE thing you could do today that would make you proud of yourself? Not "change your life," just move the needle slightly.

Minutes 10-12: Gratitude + grit One thing you're grateful for (even if it's just coffee). One hard thing you're going to face head-on today.

That's it. Twelve minutes. But if you do this for 30 days, you'll start waking up into your life instead of just surviving it.

WHY THIS ACTUALLY WORKS (THE SCIENCE PART)

Your brain is literally rewiring itself every day based on what you repeatedly think and do. Neuroscientists call this "neuroplasticity," but you can just call it "hope."

Every time you choose a different response, you're building new neural pathways.

Every time you catch yourself spiraling and redirect, you're strengthening your mental muscles.

Every time you act from your next-level identity instead of your old programming, you're becoming that person.

This isn't motivation; it's biology. And it works whether you believe in it or not.

WHAT NOBODY TELLS YOU ABOUT CHANGE

It's going to feel fake at first. That's normal.

When you start responding differently to stress, your brain will throw a tantrum. It will tell you this is stupid, you're just pretending, nothing is really changing. That's actually a good sign. It means you're disrupting old patterns.

The goal isn't to feel different immediately. The goal is to act different consistently. The feeling follows the action, not the other way around.

YOUR NEW OPERATING SYSTEM

Old OS: Life happens TO me
New OS: Life happens, I choose my response

Old OS: I need to feel motivated to act
New OS: I act to create motivation

Old OS: I am my thoughts
New OS: I have thoughts, I am not my thoughts

Old OS: Problems are punishments
New OS: Problems are puzzles

Old OS: I'll be happy when...
New OS: I'll be happy while...

THE REALITY CHECK

This won't fix everything overnight. You'll still have bad days. You'll still face real problems that positive thinking can't solve. You'll still live in a world that's often unfair, exhausting, and overwhelming.

But you'll stop being a victim of your own mind. You'll start responding instead of just reacting. And slowly, quietly, you'll become someone who can handle whatever life throws at you.

That's not just mindset work. That's freedom.

THE CHALLENGE

THE DAILY PRACTICE: FOR REAL LIFE

Every morning: 12-minute reset
Every evening: Ask yourself, "What did I do today that proves my new identity is true?"
Every week: Notice what old thought patterns tried to sneak back in
Every month: Adjust your identity statement as you grow

This isn't about perfection. This is about direction. And every day you choose to respond instead of react, you're moving toward the person you're becoming.

The best part? You don't need anyone's permission to start. You don't need to wait until you feel ready. You don't need to announce it on social media or buy special equipment.

You just need to decide: Is your mind going to run you, or are you going to run your mind?

The choice is yours. The time is now. And you're more capable than you think.

CHAPTER TEN

CREATE YOUR CODE

IF YOU DON'T CREATE YOUR CODE, YOU'LL LIVE BY SOMEONE ELSE'S.

It's 6:47 AM and you're already behind.

The coffee maker is broken, your kid can't find her backpack, and you have three missed calls from work. You haven't even left the house and you're already failing at Tuesday.

By lunch, you'll apologize for something that wasn't your fault. By 3 PM, you'll say yes to something you don't want to do. By evening, you'll scroll your phone until your eyes burn, wondering where the day went and why you feel so empty.

Sound familiar?

Here's what no one tells you: You're not broken. You're not weak. You're not failing because you lack discipline or motivation or whatever bullshit Instagram told you this week.

You're drowning because you never learned the difference between busy and productive, between reacting and responding, between surviving and actually living.

The exhaustion you feel isn't from working too hard. It's from working against yourself.

And today, that changes.

YOU'RE NOT BEHIND IN LIFE. YOU'RE BEHIND ON LIVING YOUR LIFE.

Let me guess what happened last time you tried to "get your life together":

You bought the planner. Downloaded the app. Committed to waking up at 5 AM. Lasted exactly four days before you were back to scrolling TikTok until midnight, eating cereal for dinner, and hating yourself for being "lazy."

Here's the truth nobody told you: You weren't lazy. You were operating with a broken system.

You can't discipline your way out of a life that's fundamentally misaligned with who you are. You can't motivate yourself through an existence that slowly kills your soul eight hours a day.

The problem isn't your discipline. It's that you're trying to optimize a life you never actually chose.

You already live by a code. You just don't realize it.

It shows up when you say yes to things that make you hate yourself later. When you check work emails during your kid's bedtime story. When you smile and nod while your soul screams "no." When you post strength on social media but feel soft and lost at 2 AM staring at the ceiling.

That's a code too, just not yours.

You're living by rules you didn't write:

- Be grateful for what you have (even if it's killing you)

- Don't rock the boat (even if you're drowning in it)
- Work harder (even if the work is meaningless)
- Think positive (even when your reality genuinely sucks)
- Everyone else has it figured out (spoiler: they don't)

Most people inherit their code from parents who were just trying to survive, from bosses who need you compliant, and from a society that profits from your exhaustion.

No wonder you feel like you're living someone else's life.

THE MOST DANGEROUS LIE YOU TELL YOURSELF IS "I'M FINE".

Here's what your internal dialogue actually sounds like:

"Everyone else seems to have it figured out." "I should be grateful for what I have." "I'm too old to start over." "What if I try and fail again?" "I don't deserve better." "I'm letting everyone down."

Stop lying to yourself. You're not fine.

You're tired of:

- Feeling like a fraud at work
- Snapping at people you love because you're overwhelmed
- Performing happiness on social media
- Saying "How are you?" and getting "Busy!" like it's a badge of honor
- Sunday scaries that start on Saturday afternoon
- Feeling guilty for wanting more when you "should" be grateful

The shame spiral keeps you stuck. You think the problem is you, so you try to fix yourself instead of fixing the system that's breaking you.

Here's the reality check: The reason you feel like shit isn't because you're weak. It's because you're trying to be strong in a life that doesn't fit.

STOP OPTIMIZING SOMEONE ELSE'S DEFINITION OF SUCCESS

I'm not going to insult your intelligence by telling you to "just quit your toxic job and follow your dreams." You have a mortgage. Kids. Student loans. Health insurance. I get it.

This isn't about burning your life down. It's about building something sustainable within the reality of your actual circumstances.

You don't need to quit your job to stop letting it kill your soul. You don't need to leave your relationship to stop losing yourself in it. You don't need to move to Bali to find yourself.

You need to learn how to protect your sanity within the life you actually have.

Your code isn't about becoming a different person. It's about becoming more yourself within the constraints of your real world.

SURVIVAL KIT: STOP THE BLEEDING FIRST

Before you figure out who you want to become, figure out what's killing who you are right now.

This isn't your life's purpose. This is triage.

TOOL #1: The Energy Leak Detector

You know that feeling when your phone battery dies by noon? That's your life.

Something is draining your energy faster than you can recharge it. Let's find it:

Write down:

- What makes you feel heavy before you even start?
- What do you dread checking (email, texts, bank account)?
- What conversation do you keep avoiding?
- What are you pretending is fine when it's not?

Circle the biggest energy leak. That's where we start.

Real examples from real people:

- *"I stopped checking work email after 7 PM. Not because I don't care about my job, but because I care about sleeping."*
- *"I learned to say 'I'll handle that first thing tomorrow' instead of staying up until midnight fixing problems that weren't emergencies."*
- *"I stopped saying 'How are you?' to my coworker who complains for twenty minutes every time. Now I just say 'Good morning' and keep walking."*

TOOL #2: The Stop Doing List

Everyone gives you more to do. Nobody tells you what to stop doing.

Write down:

- **What you'll stop saying yes to** (overtime you won't get paid for, plans that drain you, conversations that go nowhere)
- **What you'll stop feeling guilty about** (not answering texts immediately, taking lunch breaks, wanting time alone)
- **What you'll stop explaining or defending** (your boundaries, your decisions, your needs)

Start with one item from each category. Practice this week.

TOOL #3: The Monday Morning Reality Check

Every Sunday night, ask yourself:

- What do I actually have energy for this week?
- What can I not do and still be okay?
- What one thing would make this week feel less chaotic?

Plan for your actual capacity, not your ideal capacity.

YOU CAN'T HATE YOURSELF INTO A VERSION OF YOURSELF YOU LOVE

Here's where most self-help gets it wrong: They assume you need more discipline when what you really need is more self-compassion.

You will have days when you forget who you're trying to become. That's not failure. That's Tuesday.

You will mess up. You will revert to old patterns. You will disappoint yourself.

And that's when your code matters most (not when life is easy, but when you're tired, stressed, and everything feels impossible).

Your code isn't a jail cell. It's a safety net. It catches you when you fall so you don't have to start over from zero every time.

BUILDING YOUR CODE: THE FOUNDATION

Once you've stopped the bleeding, you can start building.

Your code has three levels:

Level 1: Boundaries (What Will I Stop Tolerating?)

- I don't argue with people who aren't listening
- I don't explain my NO more than once
- I don't carry other people's emotions for them

- I don't accept being spoken to with disrespect

Level 2: Consistency (What One Thing Will I Do Daily?)

Not twenty things. One thing you can do even on your worst day.

- I take ten minutes alone every morning before I check my phone
- I ask "How was your day?" and actually listen to the answer
- I write down one thing I'm grateful for (not toxic positivity; real gratitude)
- I end my workday at a specific time, even if everything isn't finished

Level 3: Clarity (What Do I Actually Want?)

Not what you should want. What you actually want.

- More time with people who make me laugh
- Work that doesn't make me dread Sunday nights
- A relationship where I can be myself without performance
- Enough money to stop worrying about money
- A life that feels like mine

YOUR CODE IN ACTION: REAL-WORLD EXAMPLES

These aren't Instagram-worthy moments. They're normal Wednesday decisions that compound into a different life:

- A woman stops answering "How are you?" with "Busy!" and starts saying "I'm good, how about you?" even when she's overwhelmed
- A father puts his phone in a drawer during dinner, not to be noble, but because he realized he was missing his kids' childhood while answering emails that could wait

- A manager learns to say "That's not possible with our current resources" instead of saying yes and working weekends
- A friend stops giving advice to people who just want to complain, and starts saying "That sounds really hard" instead

The Code That Fits Your Life

Your code isn't written in stone. It's written in pencil.

It changes as you change. It adapts as your circumstances adapt. The code that works when you're single won't work when you have kids. The code that works in your twenties won't work in your forties.

The point isn't to find the perfect code. The point is to have one that's yours.

Daily Code Check-In: Every morning, before you check your phone, ask:

- Who am I choosing to be today?
- What matters most when everything else is noise?
- How do I want to feel when my head hits the pillow tonight?

Not to put pressure on yourself, but to remember you have choices, even when it doesn't feel like it.

What Happens When You Start Living Your Code

You don't suddenly become fearless. You become someone who does what matters even when you're scared.

You don't stop feeling overwhelmed. You stop adding to the overwhelm.

You don't become perfect. You become consistent.

And slowly, quietly, without fanfare:

- You stop apologizing for taking up space

- You stop explaining yourself to people who don't listen anyway
- You stop waiting for permission to want what you want
- You stop performing a life and start living one

Your code becomes your anchor when everything else is chaos.

THE PERMISSION YOU'VE BEEN WAITING FOR

You don't need anyone's permission to:

- Want more than you have
- Change your mind about what you thought you wanted
- Set boundaries with people you love
- Choose yourself without feeling guilty
- Start over as many times as it takes
- Be tired and still keep going
- Take up space in your own life

You're not behind. You're not broken. You're not too late.

You're exactly where you need to be to start creating the life you actually want to live.

The person you're pretending to be is exhausting the person you actually are.

Stop performing. Start living.

Your code isn't about becoming someone else. It's about becoming more yourself.

And the world needs more people who know who they are.

```
THE CHALLENGE
```

DAILY PRACTICE: THE TWO-MINUTE CODE REMINDER

Before you check your phone each morning:

- Take two deep breaths
- Ask: "Who am I choosing to be today?"
- Pick one way you'll honor your code today
- Remember: Progress, not perfection

Start there. Everything else builds from there.

Your life is waiting for you to start living it.

CHAPTER ELEVEN

YOUR LIFE. YOUR CALL.

THE MOMENT NO ONE SAVES YOU

One day, quiet and unannounced, it happens. You wake up and realize no one is coming. No cavalry. No mentor. No promotion. No cosmic breakthrough. Just silence. Just breath. Just you. And the wreckage or resilience of every decision you've made up to now.

You feel it before you speak it. In the pit of your stomach. In the back of your throat. You look around: same four walls, same story, same delay. And this voice that used to whisper starts roaring: *This is it. Either move or die slowly inside.*

Maybe you're 32, scrolling your phone at 11:47 PM because it's the only "me time" you get between putting the kids to bed and getting up at 5:30 AM for a job that pays the bills but kills your soul piece by piece. Maybe you're 38, sitting in your car in the parking lot before work, having the same conversation with yourself you've had for three years: "I can't keep doing this, but I can't afford to stop."

Maybe you're 29, living in your childhood bedroom because rent prices are insane and student loans are a monthly reminder that your degree was supposed to be a ticket to somewhere better than this. Maybe you're 42, realizing the promotion you've been chasing for five years went to someone younger, and you're too old to start over but too young to give up.

That's the moment most people call rock bottom. But it's not. It's ignition. Because this isn't about pain; it's about clarity. That moment when you finally understand that life doesn't owe you a damn thing. That you've been waiting – waiting for a map, a coach, a push, a miracle. And none of it is coming.

That's not cruelty. That's freedom.

THE THING NO ONE TALKS ABOUT

Here's what they don't tell you about being stuck. It's not that you don't know what to do. You know exactly what to do. The problem is you're trapped between two worlds (the life you have and the life you want), and the bridge between them feels like it's on fire.

You're tired of being told to be grateful for what you have when what you have is slowly suffocating you. You feel guilty for wanting more, but you feel dead for accepting less. You're tired of financial gurus who've never had to choose between buying groceries and paying for your kid's school supplies telling you to "invest in yourself."

You're tired of productivity experts who don't understand that your "morning routine" is making sure everyone else in your house has what they need before you sprint to a job where you smile and say "everything's fine" while your dreams rot in the corner of your mind.

If you've ever felt like you're living someone else's life while your real life waits in some unreachable future, this is for you.

If you've ever sat in your car after work, too drained to walk into your own house because you know the second you do, everyone will need something from you, this is for you.

If you've ever looked at your bank account and realized that even doing everything "right" isn't enough anymore, this is for you.

THE ENERGY CRISIS THEY DON'T ADDRESS

Let's be real about something. You're not lazy. You're not weak. You're not lacking motivation. You're operating on fumes, and every self-help book you've picked up assumes you have energy reserves you burned through years ago.

You don't need someone to tell you to wake up at 5 AM when you're already up at 5 AM dealing with a toddler who thinks sleep is optional. You don't need someone to tell you to "just start" when you've started seventeen different things and life interrupted every single one.

You need strategy for when you're running on empty and still have to change everything.

Here's what I learned from talking to hundreds of people who actually made the leap: they didn't need more motivation. They needed more honesty about what change looks like when you're already maxed out.

MELISSA'S STORY

Single mom, two jobs, nursing school at night. Everyone told her to "just push through" until she had her degree. But push through what? She was already pushing. She was drowning in the push. What she needed was permission to change the game, not just play it harder.

She started small. Not with some grand business plan, but with one hour. One hour on Saturday mornings when her ex had the kids. She started a

---

meal prep service from her kitchen. Five customers. Then ten. Then twenty.

Two years later, she wasn't working two jobs anymore. She was working one, and that's hers. Not because she found some magical energy source, but because she redirected the energy she was already burning on other people's dreams toward her own.

THE FAMILY HOSTAGE SITUATION

The hardest prison isn't circumstances; it's being responsible for others while your own dreams suffocate in silence. You tell yourself you're being noble, putting everyone else first. But here's what they don't tell you: modeling mediocrity isn't protecting anyone.

Your kids don't need you to be perfect. They need you to be powerful. They need to see what it looks like when someone refuses to settle. When someone fights for the life they actually want instead of just surviving the one they have.

Your partner doesn't need you to be safe. He needs you to be alive. To be someone who hasn't given up on becoming who they're meant to be.

The guilt is real. "Who am I to want more when others have less?" "What if I fail and make things worse for everyone?" "What if I'm being selfish?"

Here's the truth that took me years to understand: selfishness is staying small when you could be contributing something bigger to the world. Selfishness is wasting your potential because it feels safer than risking failure.

NO PERMISSION SLIP, JUST CHOICE (THE REAL VERSION)

Here's the truth you already know deep down: nobody is coming to give you permission. There is no round of applause for deciding not to waste your potential. There is no green light from heaven. There's just you, and choice.

But here's what the other books won't tell you: you don't need permission, but you do need strategy. You do need a plan that works with your real life, not some fantasy version where you have unlimited time and money.

EDDIE'S STORY

Warehouse worker, night shift, three kids, mortgage underwater after the divorce. Forty-one years old and feeling like life was over. Everyone told him to "just be grateful for steady work."

But steady work that steadily kills you isn't something to be grateful for.

He didn't quit his job. He couldn't. But he started recording voice notes on his phone during his lunch breaks. Thoughts about life, about struggle, about what it really takes to change when you're already drowning. Started posting them online.

Eighteen months later, companies were paying him to speak to their employees about resilience. Not because he had it all figured out, but because he was figuring it out in real time, with real constraints, in front of real people who felt just as trapped as he used to.

He didn't need permission to start. He needed permission to believe that his struggle had value. That his voice mattered. That someone else needed to hear exactly what he was going through.

BUILDING POWER IN SILENCE

You want to know the difference between people who break through and people who break down? People who break through build power in silence while everyone else broadcasts their intentions.

They don't announce their plans at family dinner. They don't post about their "journey" on social media. They don't wait for encouragement or accountability partners.

They build. Quietly. Relentlessly. One small decision at a time.

5:30 AM: While everyone sleeps, they write.

Lunch break: While everyone scrolls, they learn.

After bedtime stories: While everyone watches Netflix, they create.

Not because they have superhuman discipline, but because they understand something crucial: the life you want is built in the margins of the life you have.

JESSICA'S REALITY

Customer service rep by day, anxiety disorder since college, caring for aging parents, student loan payments that never seem to shrink. Started a blog about managing anxiety while managing everything else. Wrote for six months before anyone read it.

But she kept writing. Not because she felt like it (most days she didn't). But because she realized something: every word she wrote was proof to herself that she was more than her circumstances.

Two years later, that blog became a book. That book became speaking engagements. Those speaking engagements became a consulting business helping companies create mental health resources for employees.

She didn't escape her life. She transformed it. From the inside out.

THE BETWEEN-WORLDS STRUGGLE

You know that feeling when you're scrolling LinkedIn and see someone who started with less than you who's now living the life you dream about? That mix of inspiration and rage? That's not jealousy. That's recognition. You're seeing someone who refused to accept that their starting point was their ending point.

But here's what you don't see in their success story: the years they spent living between worlds. Having one foot in the old life and one foot in the new one. Working their day job while building something else. Smiling at family gatherings while secretly planning their escape.

Living between worlds is brutal. You don't belong in your old life anymore, but you haven't arrived at your new one yet. You're too different for where you are, but not different enough for where you're going.

The thing no one talks about: this phase can last years. And it's supposed to. You're not slow. You're not failing. You're building something strong enough to last.

DAVID'S TRUTH

Accountant by day, musician by night, for seven years. Seven years of playing coffee shops after doing tax returns. Seven years of his family asking when he was going to "get serious about his career." Seven years of feeling like he was living a double life.

Until the day he wasn't. The day his music income surpassed his accounting income wasn't a moment of celebration; it was a moment of relief. He'd been building toward it for so long, it felt inevitable.

THE ALGORITHM OF YOUR CURRENT LIFE

Here's something that will either terrify you or liberate you: your life is running on an algorithm. Every habit, every relationship, every choice you make is perfectly designed to deliver your current results.

If you're exhausted, you've built systems that exhaust you. If you're broke, you've built systems that keep you broke. If you're invisible, you've built systems that keep you invisible.

Your life isn't broken. It's built. Built to repeat exactly what you allow.

Look at your last five years:

- What did you tolerate that you shouldn't have?
- What patterns did you repeat even though they hurt?
- What opportunities did you skip because you didn't feel ready?
- What conversations did you avoid because they were uncomfortable?

That's your algorithm. That's the code your life is running on. Unless something drastic interrupts that code, the next five years will look just like the last five with slightly more regret.

According to research from the University of Scranton, 92% of people never achieve their goals. Not because they lack desire. But because they think wanting something is the same as building toward it.

The brutal truth: if you're tired, stuck, or running in circles, it's because you've engineered it that way. Unconsciously, maybe, but completely.

So unbuild it. One micro-decision at a time. One pattern at a time. One morning you get up ten minutes earlier. One conversation you have that you've been avoiding. One boundary you set that you should have set years ago.

THE STORY THAT CHANGES EVERYTHING

There was a woman who worked as a medical assistant in a clinic that treated her like she was replaceable because, in their minds, she was. Single mom to two teenagers, divorced from a man who paid child support when he felt like it. Living in an apartment she couldn't afford to leave because she couldn't afford to move.

Every night, she'd sit at her kitchen table after her kids went to bed, stare at a stack of bills she couldn't pay, and feel like she was drowning in slow motion.

She had no plan. No savings. No business idea. Just bitterness and the stubborn refusal to let her kids watch her give up.

One Thursday night, while paying bills she didn't have money for, she muttered the words that would change everything:

"No one is coming to save me. So I'm going to become the woman I wish someone had been for me."

She started small. Not with some grand business plan, but with observation. She noticed that half the patients at the clinic were stressed about the same things she was: medical bills, insurance confusion, prescription costs.

She started helping, unofficially of course. Showing people how to apply for assistance programs. How to negotiate payment plans. How to find generic alternatives. How to navigate the system that seemed designed to confuse them.

Word spread. People started asking for her by name. Patients started bringing friends just to talk to her.

That's when she realized: her struggle had given her expertise. Her pain had given her purpose.

She got certified as a patient advocate. Started offering services on weekends. Built a client base of people who needed someone who understood their world because she'd lived it.

Three years later, she wasn't clocking in at the clinic anymore. She was running her own practice, helping families navigate medical crises while earning more than she'd ever made in her life.

She didn't inherit that life. She earned it because she made the decision that the woman she was didn't have to be the woman who died broke and hopeless.

WHAT HAPPENS WHEN YOU ACTUALLY GRAB LIFE

Everything changes.

You stop explaining yourself to people who aren't paying your bills. You stop asking for permission from people who benefit from your smallness. You stop waiting for conditions to be perfect before you make a move.

You become someone who:

- Speaks with conviction, not apology
- Moves with urgency, not excuses
- Protects their energy like it's their most valuable asset
- Makes decisions based on their future, not their past
- Shows up for themselves the way they show up for everyone else

You won't be perfect. You'll still stumble. But you'll never fold the same way again. Because once you grab life by the throat, you realize something that changes everything: *you were never stuck. You were just scared of disappointing people who weren't even paying attention.*

THE REAL FINAL HIT

You know what separates people who change their lives from people who just think about changing their lives?

They stop making their struggles sound prettier than they are.

They stop calling their dead-end job "stable." They stop calling their toxic relationship "complicated." They stop calling their financial stress "temporary." They stop calling their exhaustion "busy."

They call it what it is: unacceptable.

And once you call something unacceptable, you can't unknow it. You can't unsee it. You can't go back to pretending it's fine.

That's when everything shifts. Not because you suddenly have more time or money or energy. But because you finally have something more powerful: clarity about what you will and won't accept from your own life.

YOUR TURN

You're still reading.

That means something cracked open. You're not pretending anymore. You're not nodding politely through your own mediocrity. You're ready. Not in the fairy tale way. In the gritty, tired, honest way.

You're done with the old story. You're done asking for approval from people who aren't living your life. You're done watching others build lives they don't have to apologize for while you settle for leftovers.

Now it's your turn. Not to prove something to them. But to become something for you.

Say it. Mean it. Live it.

"They counted me out because I started behind. That's why I'm dangerous, because I had to build power in silence. Now they can't stop what they never saw coming."

The woman sitting in her car before work, wondering if this is all there is? She's about to find out she was wrong.

The man scrolling job postings at 1 AM, feeling like he's too old to start over? He's about to discover he's exactly the right age to get serious.

The parent who put everyone else's dreams first for so long they forgot they had their own? They're about to remember.

Your time isn't coming.

Your time is here.

Now move.

CHAPTER TWELVE

WHERE WE GO FROM HERE

THE LINE BETWEEN LIVING AND LYING TO YOURSELF

This isn't the end of the book. It's the beginning of your escape.

YOU'RE NOT STUCK. YOU'RE UNDECIDED.

Let's kill the biggest lie first: Nobody is stuck. That's the illusion you've sold yourself so long it started to sound like truth. But it's not true. It's paralysis masquerading as a fact.

I know this because I spent two years telling myself I was "figuring things out" while scrolling through job boards at midnight, eating leftover pizza, wondering why everyone else seemed to have their shit together. I called it being "strategic." Really, I was just terrified of letting go of who I thought I was supposed to be.

People say they're stuck when the next step terrifies them. People say they're lost when they're really just afraid to disappoint the version of themselves they've been performing for others.

The truth? You're not stuck. You're undecided. You're still negotiating with a life that's slowly killing you, pretending your quiet desperation is just "being responsible." But comfort isn't safety; it's a slow-motion prison sentence.

Here's what I wish someone had told me: **"Stuck" isn't a state; it's a decision you keep postponing.**

You've read this far. You've walked through the fire of eleven chapters. Now, you don't get to pretend you don't know. You know. You just haven't acted. Yet.

THE MOMENT OF TRUTH ISN'T A MOMENT. IT'S A CHOICE.

People wait for the breakthrough. For the divine spark. For Mercury to be in retrograde or whatever cosmic permission slip they think they need. They think change shows up like lightning: dramatic, unmistakable, impossible to ignore.

It doesn't.

It shows up on a Tuesday at 6:47 AM when you're staring at your alarm, realizing you can't stomach another day of pretending this is enough. It shows up when you're sick of your own excuses. When you make a decision in the shower, in your car, in the grocery store checkout line. One that nobody claps for, one that you commit to when you're exhausted and overlooked.

Change isn't loud. It's not a motivational quote. It's not a video that goes viral.

It's a quiet decision that you have to remake every single day until it becomes who you are.

Real transformation looks nothing like the movies. It's you staring into your bank account, your calendar, your reflection, and realizing the version of you you're trying to build won't come from scattered effort and emotional hype. It comes from systems that work even when you don't feel like it.

You don't need another pep talk. You need an escape plan. One built for your actual life, not the life Instagram thinks you should have.

◉ HOW PEOPLE ACTUALLY BREAK FREE

GROUND YOURSELF IN BRUTAL REALITY

You are not where you are by accident. Every "I'll start Monday." Every "After the holidays." Every "When things settle down." You chose this with a thousand small surrenders.

This part stings. I get it. When I finally did this inventory, I wanted to burn the list. But here's the thing: when you own it, you can change it. And this is where victims become builders.

Take inventory. Right now. No sugar-coating:

- What's actually in your bank account? (Not what you tell people; what's real)

- Who's in your inner circle? (Are they lifting you up or holding you back?)

- What time do you actually wake up? (Not when your alarm goes off; when you get up)

- What are you tolerating that you'd never let someone you love endure?

- What do you complain about but never change?

This isn't self-flagellation. This is radical ownership. The difference between people who break generational cycles and people who repeat them comes down to one thing: taking responsibility for the whole messy truth.

USE A DAILY DECISION FRAMEWORK

Forget vision boards gathering dust on Pinterest. Forget five-year plans you'll never look at again. Start here: every single morning, ask yourself:

- **What will my future self thank me for today?**
- **What am I doing that's keeping me trapped?**
- **What am I tolerating that I would never allow someone I love to tolerate?**

Write it. Say it out loud. Answer it honestly.

Because identity isn't created in your head during meditation retreats. It's built through your patterns. And patterns are built through daily, deliberate decisions that nobody sees but everybody eventually feels.

PICK ONE LANE

Confusion is a luxury you can't afford anymore. You don't need to know everything. You need to pick one direction and run like your life depends on it, because it does.

Here are the four real roads out:

1. **Start Something**: a side business, a creative project, a skill that pays, a routine that builds you
2. **Fix Something**: your finances, your health, your living situation, your boundaries
3. **Leave Something**: a toxic relationship, a soul-crushing job, a belief that's killing your dreams
4. **Learn Something**: a trade, a skill, a language that shifts your value in the marketplace

Pick one. Own it completely. Stay with it until you've earned the right to choose the next.

And if you're sitting there thinking "But I'm 35" or "But I'm 42" or "But I have kids," listen: A 2018 study by Indeed revealed that the average age for career change in the U.S. is 39. Not 22. Not 30. **Thirty-nine.** Real reinvention doesn't follow society's timeline; it follows your breaking point.

STACK MICRO-MOMENTUM

Forget massive overhauls. That's fantasy thinking that keeps you stuck.

You build real change with small wins, stacked daily. Your brain rewards completion, not perfection. Want to feel alive again? Start by showing up for yourself in ways that count.

Three non-negotiable anchors:

- **Wake up at the same time.** Even weekends. It builds neural trust with yourself.
- **Write tomorrow's plan today.** Decision fatigue is real. Beat it before it beats you.
- **Do something uncomfortable before noon.** It gives you momentum that carries through everything else.

These aren't tasks on a to-do list. These are identity builders. They're the difference between someone who talks about change and someone who embodies it.

BUILD YOUR ESCAPE PLAN

Don't make it pretty. Make it real.

On a piece of paper, answer these right now:

- **One thing I'm building:** _____
- **One thing I'm leaving behind:** _____

- **One person I'm learning from:** _____
- **One painful truth I'm owning:** _____
- **One step I'm taking this week:** _____

Stick it where you can't avoid it. Bathroom mirror. Car dashboard. Bedroom wall. Let it remind you who you're becoming.

MAKE IT REAL BY MAKING IT PUBLIC

Stop playing secret agent with your transformation. You're not mysterious; you're scared. People who say "I'm private about my goals" are usually just terrified of failing in public.

Here's the truth: **Visibility creates accountability.**

- Send one text announcing what you're building
- Share the change you're making with someone who matters
- Start a notebook called "Who I'm Becoming" and fill it

Social psychologists call it the "commitment effect." Once you declare your path, you're 65% more likely to follow through. Your shame is keeping you stuck. Use it as fuel instead.

🚨 THE FOCUS YOU NEED RIGHT NOW

You know that person you've met (in dating, business, life) who was so focused on their mission that you felt like an interruption?

They weren't rude. They were just done settling. They'd sit you down and say, "It's not that I don't care about this. It's that I've had enough of life's bullshit. And nothing (not even something good) is getting in my way right now."

That's the kind of focus you need. Not balanced. Not polite. **Obsessed.**

You don't need work-life balance. You need work-life integration around the person you're becoming. Everything else is noise.

WHAT YOU OWN, YOU CAN CHANGE

Ownership is the leverage most people avoid because it's terrifying. But it's also the only door to actual power.

Own the habits that stole your time. Own the dreams you shelved for "someday." Own the version of you that stayed quiet to keep the peace. Own the recovery.

I spent three years blaming my industry, my boss, and my circumstances for feeling trapped. The day I stopped pointing fingers and started pointing at myself in the mirror, that's when everything shifted.

WHERE LIFE ACTUALLY HURTS

Pain doesn't live in mediocrity. Pain lives where truth threatens comfort.

Life doesn't hurt when you:

- Keep the job that pays the bills but kills your soul
- Keep the peace by never speaking up
- Keep the mask that everyone expects to see

It hurts when you:

- Quit without a backup plan because you can't fake it one more day
- Say "no more" to people who've taken you for granted
- Walk away from guaranteed misery toward uncertain possibility

That Sunday night anxiety? That's not random. That's your soul trying to tell you something. Listen to it.

THE FINAL SECTION: STOP ASKING. START MOVING.

You don't need another mentor. You don't need a course, a hack, a shortcut, or someone else's permission.

You need movement.

Move scared. Move confused. Move while your hands are shaking and your bank account is screaming. Move before you're ready, because you'll never feel ready.

The path reveals itself to those who walk it, not to those who plan it to death.

Motion creates meaning. Momentum is born from mess.

FINAL QUESTION: WHERE WILL YOU BE IN FIVE YEARS?

Look at the last five years of your life:

- What did you build that you're proud of?
- What patterns did you repeat that kept you small?
- What opportunities did you let fear talk you out of?

That's your trajectory, unless you change it.

The Bureau of Labor Statistics says most people switch jobs 12 times in their lifetime. Most of those changes weren't planned. They happened because of pain. Layoffs. Burnout. Breaking points.

Translation: Most people don't have it figured out. They just move when staying still becomes more painful than the unknown.

So here's your choice: **Move by design, or move by desperation.**

This is it. The last line before the new life begins:

"From this page forward, I build. I move. I own. I become."

You're not the hero they expected. You're the one they underestimated.

The underestimated rise with purpose. And now?

You don't just grab life by the balls. You take back every year you gave away to fear.

The question isn't whether you can do this. The question is: How much longer can you afford not to?

Still not sure what that first step looks like? Take one anyway.

The path doesn't reveal itself to the prepared; it reveals itself to the committed.

Most successful people didn't know what they were doing when they started.

They figured it out by starting.

If this book spoke to you, don't keep it to yourself. Share it. Pass it on and when you're ready, leave a review online so others know they're not alone in their struggle either.

Your voice helps this message travel farther than these pages ever could.